CLOUDS OF TIME
AND OTHER STORIES

by
John Williams

D1610622

GWASG CARREG GWALCH

ISBN: 0-86381-115-9

Cyhoeddir gyda chymorth ariannol
Cyngor y Celfyddydau.

Published with financial aid
from the Arts Council.

Cover & illustrations: ANNE MORRIS

First published in 1989 by Gwasg Carreg Gwalch,
Capel Garmon, Llanrwst, Gwynedd,
Wales.
Tel: 06902 261

"But new furrows are ploughed in old fields, harvests are sown and gathered and names that sprang from the red earth itself have died away to a faint murmur which only native ears attuned may hear."

Margiad Evans,   'Country Dance'

CONTENTS

Introduction 6
Clouds of Time 9

Skin Deep 59
The Guest 65
Trotters 70
On a Shining Night 75
Into the Mist 80
Gleaners' Harvest 85
The Big Water 90
Cock up! 96
Stones and Snookers 102
Home Killed or Cured 107
Small Mercies 112
Over the hills & Far Away 121

THE AUTHOR

John Ellis Williams was born in Llanddeiniolen, North Wales in 1924. He is of farming stock and was in the RAF during the war. After the Liberation he was attracted by the Existentialist movement in Paris where he became friendly with Simone de Beauvoir. Later, he tramped the Marches in the company of vagrants and gypsies.

With his wife he took a motor cycle on a winter's journey across Europe to Cape St Vincent from where they retraced George Borrow's itinerary through the Iberian Peninsula, living with Portuguese fishermen and the troglodyte gypsies of Andalusia in the caves of the Sacro Monte at Granada.

He has also spent periods in the Basque Country and in the Camargue, and he has walked extensively in the Sierra Nevada, in the foothills of the Matterhorn, and the Alps around Chamonix.

He has published seven novels in Welsh, and has written for radio and TV in both languages. He has one son who is a law student in England.

'Clouds of Time' was serialised in Welsh in the woman's magazine *Pais*, and most of the stories first appeared in Welsh in *Eco'r Wyddfa*.

'Skin Deep', 'Trotters', 'On a Shining Night', and 'The Guest' were read on BBC Radio Wales. 'Gleaners' Harvest' was the Radio 4 Morning Story.

'The Big Water', 'Into the Mist', 'Over the Hills', 'Home Killed or Cured', and 'Stones and Snookers' have appeared in *The Countryman*.

'Small Mercies' was shown on BBC Wales TV.

INTRODUCTION

These stories first came to my notice when I read five of them on the radio, (one as the Morning Story). And what struck me about them, apart from their ease of reading, was the realisation, that the style in which they are written, is the nearest thing to writing 'Welsh in English'; a direct result, so I'm told, of the author's long practice of composing syntax concurrently in both languages.

The material revolves around the lives of his parents, who were members of the farming fraternity that survived by 'making marsh into meadow' on the marginal heathland on the floor of Llanddeiniolen parish between Menai and Eryri, when the 'motive power' as he says, 'was shared by the horses and the water-wheel, and where we were fairly secure within the fabric of our own community, when codes were rigid, and based on good-will and the division of capital, where neighbours sent men and implements to help with the seasonal activities, and even maids were leant and borrowed, and interest in kind paid for their services. Favours were recorded and returned, either in one piece or by instalments. It was pretty near a *soviet* in its own unwitting way, operating in what was left of the Feudal System'.

The stories by their very nature are a document of the period between the wars in the North Wales agrarian communities. But they are also conductors of feeling; warmth and nearness, alternating with shivers of soul-penetrating cold — the narrative constantly swinging between tenderness and brutality and eruptions of violence; depicting not only the melange of ingredients that constituted survival on the land in those austere times, but reminding us of the continuity of the Celtic character and its composition, and the people who centuries before, had lived on the same land, and constructed the Iron Age fort, under the shadow of which the author spent his early years — a geographical feature which not only dominated the surrounding landscape, but his awareness as well.

But humour — albeit often amongst tragedy — is ever present, sharpening the focus; mesmerising the reader into imagining that it's not cold print that he has before him, but a flesh and blood story-teller, such as the ones who shared the hearths on winter nights in the farmhouses and the cottages of Wales.

The book, incorporating as it does, the romance of the courtship of John Williams' parents, and how they sheltered a deserter from the trenches, and the effect a far away war can have on a secluded community, will be read as long as people are drawn to value their traditions, and in discovering how things were 'in the long ago time'.

Meredith Edwards
Cilcain, Clwyd

At the servants' ball

CLOUDS OF TIME

ONE

It's not an easy thing for a man to tell a woman's story, especially when she is his own mother, and I don't know *everything* about Agnes — we called each other by our Christian names — other than what she saw fit to tell me, and snatches of information that came my way unwittingly from those who are always eager to acquaint a man with his pedigree. But if it is to be told, I'm the one to try. There's no one else left to tell it now.

Had I been a daughter, I would, no doubt have got to know more, but all the same, we could be close sometimes. "When you're eighteen," she used to say, "you're going to live for ever. Life is like a book. Some chapters make you want to go on, others bog you down."

She started work at eleven in the Grand Lodge at Faenol Hall. Her mother was dead then, and my grand-father was left with four of them. Her departure meant that there was one mouth less to feed.

She lived with an old couple at the Lodge. She helped the old lady with the housework, and she collected sticks in the park and fed the ducks. The old man, besides tending his bit of garden had to open and close the main gates for the carriages, and rake the gravel back into the tracks and hoof-marks.

She was only four miles away from home, but she had bouts of homesickness, and she said she used to cling to the bars of the gates and push her head in between, longing to go through and return to her family at the cottage by the church in Llanddeiniolen. Even now, when I pass those gates, I see that little fair-haired maid peering at me through the bars.

Later, she went to look after a family in a vicarage in the Conwy Valley. She liked it there; there was a thoroughly Welsh atmosphere. The only drawback was that she was further from home; she couldn't get to see her family so often.

My grand-father was ageing early, as people did then. He

worked in the Bluestone Quarry at Dinorwig, hanging in a rope against the cliff-face in all weathers, boring shot-holes. He had mistimed a fuse once, and one side of his face was peppered with pinhead holes. He was Vicar's warden at the Old Church, and his son, Rolant, who was his very image, my mother said, was already working in the quarry at fifteen.

He was the second Rolant. The other had died in infancy as many children did. The name Rolant has not been a fortunate one for the family, and none of the descendants has been so free of superstition as to adopt it.

The Great War had been going on then for over a year, and Siôn, the eldest boy was in France, God knew where, and from time to time, news of battles lost and won filtered through to the parish. They were all very anxious about him.

Then there was Ruth, the little sister, still at the Church School. In between her bouts of play she pretended to keep house, but she was already afflicted with the scourge of the quarrying community: she would lie on her bed for hours coughing her consumptive lungs dry.

It was in May of that year that things began to go wrong for Agnes. On a bright morning she was spreading out clothes to air in the vicarage garden, when she saw a large policeman cycling up the drive. The police hardly ever called upon anyone then unless it was on a serious errand. Minor matters were settled among people themselves.

When Agnes saw him, her arm tightened round her clothes-basket. He asked for Agnes Jones by name. "I've got bad news for you girl," he said. "You are to go home at once, your brother has been killed."

Agnes felt an icy tingling through her shoulders. Her body folded like a jack-knife, and the basket rolled away from her. When she recovered, she was lying on the sofa in the vicarage, and the vicar's wife was bending over her. The policeman seemed to have disappeared.

"How did ...?" She was going to ask something, but they would not allow her to talk. Later, the vicar explained that the policeman could not stay: he had to go to the village to tell some woman that her husband was missing. The effects of the war were beginning to penetrate the Welsh countryside.

In the afternoon, the vicar took Agnes to the station at Conwy in the governess cart. As she travelled in the train parallel to the coast, she looked to seaward and saw the Seiriol lighthouse and Anglesey, and they looked out of character in the sun-light. By tea time she was climbing the hill from Felinheli. The broom was yellow she said, and the bees were humming in the hedge bottoms, and she could not understand why everything was going on so unheeding while her brother was dead in France.

Just then she heard the sound of hooves, and there appeared round the corner Bob Mul, the parsonage servant, with the dog cart and Jini Wen the pony. In spite of the heat he was wearing his thick fustian clothes and his black hat.

"How are you girl?" he said. "I came looking for you as soon as I could." He stepped down and led the pony round.

They said hardly anything to each other as they came up the road, side by side on the bench, but Bob spoke at last, because it had to be got over with sometime:

"He took too much upon himself you see, like we are all apt to do at times, and there was no one happening to be at hand."

"What do you mean?" asked Agnes.

Bob flicked the reins against the pony's rump.

"Didn't anybody tell you?"

"No. I know nothing."

"Well — he went over the top with the tipping waggon you see."

"Siôn?" Agnes shouted. "In France?"

Bob pulled the pony up in the middle of the road.

"Siôn?" he said. "It's about Rolant I'm talking, girl."

Agnes turned to face him. "Rolant? Rolant? But he is only a little boy. In the quarry was Rolant, not in the war." She dropped her head on her knees and sobbed.

They went past the Old Church and the school, and when they got to the cottage gate, it was much too soon for Agnes.

"Wait Bob," she said, and she went to the cast-iron water-pump that stood in the hedge. She rolled up her sleeves, and put one hand under the spout, and as she worked the handle with the other, and laved her face, she suddenly remembered how they ran there on their way from school, taking turns to pump water into each other's hands.

There were several people in the house when she went in, offering help and company and condolences as was the rural way. My grand-father was sitting in his high armchair with his gold watch-chain across his waistcoat and clad in his Sunday best, looking like a stranger in his own home. He took hold of my mother's forearms.

"You've come at a strange time girl."

In the milk-house scalding the dairy utensils was Mari Lewis, Rynys Lwyd, their neighbour across the fields. She was old, and she had a wide experience of being in attendance on death and of dealing with sorrowing families across the parish. And Agnes' best friend was there too, Elin, Pen Rhyd, another neighbour who lived in the smallholding that snuggled in the lee of the old Celtic Fort. Agnes felt better at seeing her.

"Where's Ruth?" asked my mother.

My grand-father looked in the direction of the bedchamber door. "She's in there, day and night. See if you can't persuade her to come out."

Mari Lewis had come into the living kitchen; she carried a small basin with pieces of dry bread in it, and Agnes said,

"How are you Mari Lewis?"

"I'm better than if I was worse. Listen, I'll come with you now to make him some sinner's bread."

Agnes stiffened and faced her.

"Oh no you won't." She put her back to the chamber door and turned the knob and backed inside.

"What's come over the girl?" asked Mari of Elin, but Elin said nothing only looked at my grand-father for answer. And he said at last,

"Agnes is the boss now she's come. I've got no one else."

Mari returned to the milk-house and closed the door on herself.

After making sure that Mari was not following her, Agnes went into the small bedchamber. I don't know whether she was prepared for what she saw there. Ruth was sitting in a chair at the foot of the bed on which was laid a long bundle covered with a sheet.

"What are you doing here Ruth?" Mother asked.

The girl did not answer, nor did she once take her eyes off the bundle on the bed. My mother said that a peculiar feeling had overcome her too; a feeling of tranquility and strength at the same time. She said no more. She drew out her hatpin and laid her hat on the bed, then she took off her coat very slowly, as if she had just arrived from Morning Prayer, and was getting herself ready to prepare the dinner. She took hold then of the corner of the sheet and drew it slowly off the bundle on the bed.

Rolant was lying with his eyes closed and his arms folded; and his coat sleeve was covered in slate dust, and it had been ripped until part of his naked arm was visible, dark now, with the stilled blood. On his temple there was a deep gash, and a sliver of slate stuck out of it, mixed with the congealed blood. Agnes swayed and replaced the cover.

"Have you had anything to eat Ruth?"

"I don't want anything."

"Come, I'll make you some bread and milk." She took hold of her sister's forearm. "Come, that's a good girl."

"I want to look after Rolant."

"You can come back after. He wouldn't want you to be without food would he? He'd prefer to be on his own for a bit."

"Do you think so Agnes?"

"Yes, come now."

Ruth allowed herself to be persuaded. They both went into the living kitchen.

"Who is going to look after him, father?" asked Agnes.

"Griffith Jones, the joiner. He should have come by now."

"I'm not going to let Rolant be like that for a minute longer," said Agnes. "I'm going to look for Griffith Jones now."

"I'll come with you for company," said Elin.

They set out past Pen Rhyd, through Tan Dinas Hollow, and then they climbed the hill past the Old Fort, where, it was said, the silhouette of a warrior with his shield and spear stood upon the ramparts against the sunset every eve of the Feast of Beltane. When they came to the top, the shallow valley was in front of them, leading off, and gradually rising to the foothills of Snowdon and the Bluestone Quarry.

"You did right with Mari Lewis," said Elin suddenly. "It's time she gave up some old customs like that."

"Sinner's bread?" said my mother. "Granted she did it for mother, but Rolant was too young. He didn't have any sins."

"Does she really believe in it do you think?" asked Elin.

"Oh yes. She thinks that if she puts the bread on the corpse and then eats it herself, she is taking the deceased's sins upon herself."

They said nothing for a while, until they met coming round a sudden corner, a man pushing a large chest on a hand-cart. They halted in their tracks and grasped each other's forearms. The man stopped by them and he said to Agnes.

"My dear Miss Jones. You've come to look for me, I expect. I'm so sorry, but I've got two this week you see, that's what it is."

"I see," said Agnes recovering but still staring at the coffin on the cart. "We're calling on Nantw Jones you see. My father and Mari Lewis are expecting you."

"That is good," said Griffith Jones, picking up the handles, and they could still hear the trundle of the cartwheels from a long way off.

"What do you want with Nantw Jones at this hour?" asked Elin.

"It was only an excuse," said Agnes. "I didn't want to walk back with him all the way did I?"

"What shall we do then?"

"We'll go down the Waen and double back the other way."

As they went down the Waen they saw the inhabitants out in their gardens or sitting in their doorways, enjoying the last of the summer twilight, and my mother said that she had the same feeling as the one she had coming up from Felinheli station. What right had they to be doing that while Rolant was being put in his casket? But the people greeted the girls gently and with dignity.

"Terrible about your brother ... we are sorry. We'll come to see your father ... such a dear boy too, and kind."

Everyone with a good word. 'If you seek glory — die' thought Agnes, remembering the local saying.

On they went along the path through the marshes. The vapour was beginning to gather over the spongy bogs after the day's heat, and overhead in the dark sky a snipe was drumming: a sign of misfortune, coming rather late, thought Agnes in her case.

To the left, in the gloom, stood the House of Ffynnon Gegin Arthur, the chalybeate well, to which people came from far and near to alleviate their afflictions by bathing in, and drinking the water.

The young corn was shooting green in Bifan field, and the girls walked close to the wall to avoid treading on it, and just then, in front of them, they saw an object in a gateway. Elin stood transfixed grasping my mother's forearm.

"What is it?" she asked.

"Come," said Agnes, "we'll go past right quickly, but don't say a word, whatever you do."

They both stepped out into the corn out of the way.

TWO

"What do you think you're doing treading in that corn?" said a voice.

"Who's there?" asked Agnes.

A young man stepped out of the gateway with a gun under his arm.

"Never mind who I am. Who are you?"

"Is it Joss, Gors, you are?" asked Agnes.

"And it's Agnes, Llan Isa, you are. Aren't you afraid of going head first into the swinging bogs at this time of night?"

"We're going home," said Elin, recovering her nerve. "Aren't you ashamed of talking like that to someone who's had a bereavement?"

"Who like?"

"Don't you know that her brother has been killed in the quarry yesterday?"

"Killed?" said the man. "I didn't know, believe me. Rolant? Get away. I am sorry Agnes."

"Thank you," said my mother. "We'll have to go now. Are you coming Elin?"

But the boy was not so eager to let them. "Listen, wait," he said. "I'll come with you over the Dead Marsh, you might easily wander off into the bogs."

They didn't seem to have any objection then, and he walked in front of them along the narrow pathway, calling instructions over his shoulder now and again: 'Mind this' 'Watch out for that hole', and the sound of his voice was comforting to Agnes.

A curlew was calling somewhere beyond the peat hags.

"Have you heard anything from your brother Siôn?" asked Joss.

"No, not a word," said Agnes.

"Ellis, my brother is in France too."

"Siôn is with the Royal Welch, on the Somme or somewhere. It's a very bad place they say."

"A boy from Bethel was killed last week," said Elin without thinking.

"There won't be any boys left when it's all over," said Joss.

"There won't," said Agnes.

"What will you do without boys, Elin?" he asked.

"I can do without them pretty well, my lad."

"And Dafydd Fachall?" asked Agnes.

"Oh him?" said Elin, and in order to lay another scent she said to Joss. "I thought your brother was in Australia?"

"Yes, he was."

"What's he doing in France then, pray?"

"He dropped everything and came to fight for this country."

"Even after they sent him away for poaching pheasants?"

"Yes, how did you know?"

"Well, I heard that your father would have been made to leave the farm by the squire if he didn't send his son away."

She felt Agnes prodding her in the back and she desisted.

"How long has your father been dead?" asked Agnes.

"Three years. There's only mother and me, and my sister now."

By the time they were passing under the Old Fort their enthusiasm in each other's company had driven off their sorrow for a while; that mechanism in the soul, that youthful shock-absorber which wears thinner with age.

They came to the narrow stile at the top of the Harp Field. Joss took the girls' hands one by one, and he pulled them up the steep steps, and Agnes was reluctant to give him hers, but when she did, she felt the strong pull of the arm.

"We'll be all right now," she said straightening her long skirt and drawing away.

"Are you sure?" asked Joss. "There's a *bwgan* in Tan Dinas Hollow after dark, isn't there Elin?"

"Don't be silly," said Agnes. "You'll frighten the girl."

But Elin was not so sure whether she wanted to be frightened or not.

"There is something in the pond," she said, "moving on top of the water in the dark. My mother saw it one night when she was coming home from Tomos Morus' shop."

"I'll come with you," said Joss, and he hid his gun in the

16

hedge bottom. "You can't tell who is wandering about in the dark."

They walked in Indian file down Lôn-y-Gof, and when someone came to meet them they had to draw aside.

"Good night to ye," said someone with authority. "Is that ye Miss. Jones? I'm verra sorry bout yer wee brother." And before my mother could reply, the man went on. "I suppose ye didna see anyone comin' to meet ye. Thur's been poachers in the spinney."

The three stood dumb, and then they chorused, "No we didn't." The man disappeared then into the darkness.

"Scottish gamekeeper," said Joss. "There's respect for you. Talking about his own business on the same breath as offering condolences. I hope the old stoat doesn't catch any of them. Good thing I didn't bring the gun."

They came to the big broom bush by the bend from where they could look down into the shallow valley.

"There's a light in your house," said Joss.

"There's one in the church too, look," said Elin. "Funny, they'd cancelled the children's meeting."

"It's John Williams the sexton," said Agnes, "making ready for..." and she said no more.

They went through Tan Dinas Hollow and none of them said a word. But when they got to Pen Rhyd gate Agnes said:

"There you are, Elin. Don't come any further. Your mother will be wondering."

"Are you sure?" asked Elin.

"Yes, I'm sure." They held on to each other for a minute.

"I'll come tomorrow first thing after the milking." And when she was turning to go, Elin added: "We didn't see the *bwgan* after all."

"He must have known that I was with you," said Joss.

Agnes allowed the boy to come with her as far as Llan Isa gate.

"Tell me, Agnes," he said, "have you got someone with you taking charge?"

"My father, you know. He's seen more than one being killed in the quarry."

"Yes, but not his own son, dear girl, has he? Who is going to carry the bier and things like that. You'll have to get someone you know."

17

"The quarrymen will all be there you see," explained Agnes. "We won't have to do a thing."

"I suppose you're right. It's an advantage to belong to a community like that when you are in a corner. I'll come and see your father tomorrow."

"Come now with me."

"Oh no, I'm not dressed for it."

They had reached the pump then and they stood facing, not really knowing what to say next.

"Agnes, before you go, I want to tell you something."

"Yes?"

"I haven't told anyone else you understand."

"What is it you want to tell?"

"Someone has — has sent me a white feather."

"A white feather? For you? But you can't go to the war. You've got to help your mother look after the farm. Who would be so cruel? And besides, your brother is in the thick of it."

"I don't know," said Joss lowering his head.

"Look now," said my mother, putting her hand boldly on his arm. "Promise me now. Don't think any more about it — will you?"

"If you say so. Will you do something else for me?"

"What now, again?"

"Will you pump some water for me? I'm choking for a drink. We had red herring for tea. They want to swim."

They went on to the step and Agnes got hold of the handle and began to pump water into the boy's cupped hands.

"It's awful to be doing this without Rolant," she said. "Do you remember how he used to race to be first?"

When they got down off the step, Joss said. "I'll be coming to the funeral."

"I know."

"If you should need anything, will you send word?"

"I'm sure to," said Agnes, "and thank you for coming with us. It was comforting to have company." And she felt his large wet hand grasping hers.

I never heard my mother say much about her brother's funeral, and by now I realise why. It was too much of an ordeal for her to keep in mind. There must be some mechanism in the soul too, at such times, to numb the nerve-ends. But she mentioned one thing I remember, and it only added to her sorrow.

18

She had to rummage through that old tin box to find the necessary documents, only to find the joiner's bill for the other Rolant. I have it still.

'John Rowland Jones to Griffith Jones, Arthur Terrace. For making a pine coffin for his little child: sixteen shillings.'

But I heard tell from other people who were there at the time.

Neither my grand-father nor his daughters had to lift a finger throughout that week. Elin came to make the meals and clean, and milk the cows. Mother did nothing but sit in the front room, receiving people and shaking hands with dozens and dozens. A gang of children came after school asking to be let in to see the deceased. Then she went with Ruth and Elin to the Golden Goat in Caernarfon to buy mourning and a new hat for Elin to come to the funeral, and Mother said that she had a talking from John Williams the sexton for taking it off and readjusting it in the church porch.

Joss came one evening in his navy-blue suit and tight trousers, with his gold chain across his waistcoat and his boots hard brushed. He put half-a-crown spending money in my grand-father's hand, a custom that ensured against anyone having a pauper's burial. Then Mother took him to see Rolant. He was lying there in his Sunday best, she said, with his prayer-book in his hand, as if he was resting before setting out for Sunday School or Morning Prayer at the Old Church. But what she regretted most, was that she could not ask Joss to sit with the family in the front room, like Elin. It just wouldn't do. It would set the whole parish talking. She had to be satisfied in farewelling with him by the pump, and going back indoors without dawdling, to receive the callers.

They said that hundreds had congregated in Llanddeiniolen Church on the day of the funeral. The Dinorwig Quarry had closed, and most of the four thousand men who worked there were choking the lane to the churchyard and spilling over into the fields. It was a warm, still day, and the scent of broom blossom filled the hedges.

Elin had spread a white damask cloth on the table in the front room, and opened out the leaves. Both doors were open to allow the people to file through the house and leave their offering on the cloth, and that took about two hours, such was their number. The bier was carried by the men from Rolant's gallery. The others all walked behind and they stood outside the church, under that ancient 'long awaiting yew tree' as W. J. Gruffydd the poet called it later.

After earthing, it took a great deal of persuasion to get Ruth to come home, but come she had to, leaving her brothers there with their mother, forever young.

The following Sunday, a memorial sermon was preached by Mr. Davies the old parson, and during the responses, he commended all the men of the parish 'who were fighting the war of the just against the forces of evil, in the trenches of the Somme and the deserts of Mesopotamia', to the Lord's safe keeping.

But in the middle of all her sorrow, something else was worrying Agnes. She had not seen Joss at all on either occasion, nor upon enquiry, had anyone else.

My grandfather with his second wife, Mother, and Ruth (on crutches).

THREE

My grand-father did not go to the quarry for a day or two, and my mother did not return to her post immediately. She walked one afternoon to Rhiwlas, on the other side, to see her grandparents and relieve her sorrow, but more than anything she wanted to know what had become of Joss.

She was not then familiar enough with the family to march there and ask. She had even tried to persuade Elin to go there on the pretext of asking for eggs to put under a broody hen.

On the return journey, she dawdled on the hill overlooking Gors Farm, but all she saw was a woman in a white apron going to the well with two pails. She could not stay overlong, however. It was the night to go to Gors Bach Inn to get the weekly groceries that Bob Mul used to leave there. Agnes was familiar at the tavern, she just lifted the latch and walked in, but she had never been in the drinking-kitchen. There was only one kind of woman to be found frequenting such a place then.

"Are there dwellers?" she called as she walked in that night, and Mrs. Jones came from the back to greet her. They sat each side of the fire, and Agnes began to give an account of her day. But it was never easy to sustain a conversation in that place. There was always someone clamouring for attention in the drinking-kitchen, and there seemed to be no shortage of dry throats that evening.

Mrs. Jones was taking her time serving, and my mother was on the point of snatching her basket and going when the landlady reappeared with astonishing news.

"There are two men from the other side in there," she said, "and they were saying that Ellis Williams, Gors Farm, has been killed with the Australians on the Somme."

Agnes looked into the fire, and her eyes moistened. She remembered what Joss had said: "There won't be any boys left."

But at least the information had put a stop to the wondering. She knew now why she had not seen Joss.

She went home in the dark hugging the churchyard wall, a place that most wayfarers avoided at that hour. But Agnes's fear of it had disappeared ever since her mother had been buried there.

My grand-father was saddened when she arrived home and told him about Ellis Williams. They both looked at each other, and the same question was in their eyes: Who will be next?

Agnes was keen to go and see the Gors family that night, although it was late.

"What if you went into the bogs?" said my grand-father.

"I'll come with you," said Ruth.

"No you won't. I'll call on Elin as I go by."

But she had no intention of calling on Elin. She went by Pen Rhyd at a great pace, but when she started to climb Lon-y-Gôf, she began to doubt her wisdom in starting. The hazel bushes hung over the walkway like a tunnel, and a broken branch was squeaking in Tan Dinas woods, but on she went, yet in the end the tension of the previous week overcame her. She sat on the stile at the top of the Harp Field and wept. It was a relieving flow of tears; and she wept for Rolant, for Siôn in the trenches, and for the bereaved Gors family. But in a minute she felt better, and on she went, across the Dead Marsh in the dark, treading from one dry tussock to the other. Suddenly she felt her feet and her calves, and then her thighs being sucked into some liquid as thick as porridge, and she was on her way to those places under the earth. She clutched at a clump of rushes, and held on like a crab, and she was shouting three loaves for a penny, when, to her relief, she saw a glimmer of light coming towards her across the marsh.

When it arrived, my mother caught a glimpse of a strapping girl carrying a stout gorse branch in her hand. She extended the branch for my mother to grasp, and there began such a struggle to get her free of the clutches of the swinging bog as had never been seen in that place; but eventually my mother came out of the morass. She was lying on the ground as helpless as a wet calf, and the big girl was panting and leaning on her branch. She soon got her wind back however and Agnes on her feet, and arm in arm they went over the slate footbridge, saying not a word to preserve their breath, and that's how they eventually arrived in Gors living kitchen, and Anne Jane Williams was aghast at the sight.

22

"In heaven's name Harriet," she said, "what have you been doing? And what's happened to this poor creature?"

Harriet however was too wise and practical to go into details. She had the big earthen basin on the slate table in the milk-house filled with hot water in two minutes, and she helped Agnes to divest and clean herself, and in no time they were both back in the living kitchen regaling the old lady with the whole story.

Anne Jane Williams had been baking that afternoon, and there was still some fire left under the wall-oven. She pushed more faggots into the fire hole and opened the oven door to let the heat out into the room. On the hob there was a large jug of linseed brew, laced with liquorice, and there was my mother, with her cup on the oven shelf, sipping that, with Joss's big coat over her shoulders, and a towel whipped round her head, looking, she thought, like the Marsh King's Daughter. She was ashamed very nearly to dying for causing the people so much trouble. They however, did not seem to mind so much. They were thanking the Lord that she was alive, and they showed their gratitude in a practical way. When Agnes had recovered enough to converse, she didn't know what on earth to say to them, because it was they after all who were the objects of sympathy.

In the end, she plucked up enough courage to mention her errand, but she didn't know, under the circumstances, whether it would be right and proper to offer sending money; she had her half-crown grasped in her palm all the time. But in spite of everything, she had something else pricking at her mind. There was no sign of Joss anywhere, and she didn't think it would be quite the thing to ask, but his whereabouts were revealed in the most casual manner, when Agnes at last suggested that it was time for her to go.

"You'll not go on your own this time girl," said Anne Jane. "Joseph has gone to a neighbour to lend a hand with some work, he'll be back just now. I'll have him take you."

So it was settled. Mother took another drink of linseed, and she set it on the oven shelf as if she was paying rent for the whole place, but she just could not understand why the two women could be so complacent, having just lost a son and brother. She came to know later, that the life of the land has to go on in the face of 'flood and famine, war and strife' and it wouldn't do for any of them to break down or show emotion of any kind.

My mother used to talk about that night until the very end, as if it had been a main crossroads in her life.

Joss arrived eventually, and his frame filled the living kitchen doorway. He didn't know what to say when he saw Agnes sitting there with his coat covering her. Then they started telling him about her escape from the swinging bog, and Anne Jane kept repeating every now and then, "And if Harriet hadn't happened to go out for more faggots and heard her..." And all the time, my mother's plight seemed to be more important than their own.

Agnes had imagined that she could have walked with Joss along the footpaths, but his mother insisted that he hook the pony in the milk-float, and take her all the way round the road, so that's how it was, and they had two candles one on either side the wash-boards, to show the way.

"Come again, don't be strange," said Anne Jane as they were setting off, "to get another cup in the oven."

"I'm sure to," said Agnes, and she knew that it would not be long, because she was going home in Harriet's clothes, a size or two too large. But it took time for her to compose herself in Joss's company as they sat side by side on the bench in between the candles. Yet, she felt that they had now a great deal in common, having each lost a brother through war and accident, and so much importance did she attach to the fact that she could not help mentioning it.

"Funny how they both went within one week," she said.

"Yes," said Joss, "but you've got more consolation about Rolant. At least you were able to bury him with dignity. We can't even do that for Ellis. He'll be wrapped in a blanket and thrown in a hole. That's all he'll matter after coming such a long way to fight."

Agnes had no ready reply, and they were silent as they descended Caerau Hill under the Old Fort.

"I feel like enlisting myself sometimes," said Joss suddenly.

"Don't be silly," said Agnes with finality. "Your mother needs you more than ever now."

They had come to Pen Rhyd gate, and Agnes could see a light in the little window and she wondered what Elin was doing, and what she would say if she happened to come out and see her riding by like a queen.

"I might even go to Australia," said Joss again.

"What would you be doing in a place like that?"

24

"Ellis had a sheep-farm in New South Wales. I suppose that will come to my mother now, but someone will have to go there to settle his affairs."

"Why must it be you then?"

"There's no one else to go, is there?"

"I'd be afraid of that old sea – I would," said Agnes. "I've never cared for the sea."

"What will you do now though?" asked Joss. "Will you go back in service?"

"There's nothing else for it is there? But I would like somewhere nearer, so that I could keep an eye on them at home."

"Where will you get a place do you think?"

"I've a mind to go and see the parson. He gets to know about places like that before anyone."

"Perhaps I'll be able to see you oftener then?"

"Not if you're in Australia, will you?"

"I shan't be staying. But tell me something else, as we are talking about your family."

"What's that?"

"What's to become of little Ruth? She seems to be coughing something terrible."

"I'm more anxious about her than I am about anything. She ought to be in a sanatorium by rights, but a place like that costs money."

Just then they saw a light coming towards them. As it approached they saw that it was a candle in a jamjar. There were two — no, three people, crowded on the side to let them by.

"Father? Ruth? — and Elin? Is that you?" Agnes called.

"What kept you so long?" asked my grand-father. "Why did you not let her come?" he asked Joss.

"She's been ..."

"Yes, her father has been terribly worried," Elin cut across.

"I'll tell you in a minute," said Agnes, stepping down from the float.

"Good night, John Rowland," said Elin, and she marched off into the darkness.

"Wait," Joss called after her. "You can come back with me."

"No thank you." Elin's voice was barely audible from the distant dark.

Agnes looked at her father and asked:
"What's got into the girl pray?"

The author's parents.

FOUR

My grand-father did not offer any excuses for Elin's behaviour until Joss had turned about and gone.

"Well, what do you expect?" he asked as they made their way back to the house. "The girl came to look for you, and I thought that you ..."

"Had called to ask her to come with me," said Agnes.

"That's right, and we started to worry didn't we? You shouldn't be doing silly things like that at your age."

"I won't do it again," said Mother, like a child caught in mischief, but the assurance did not seem to satisfy her father.

"I hope you won't. And what does that boy mean, keeping you out until this hour? I would have told him too if he hadn't just been through a bereavement."

But whatever it was that had upset Elin, it passed very quickly. In a couple of days she was running down the road in her apron with dough sticking to her elbows, and she was waving a piece of paper in her hand.

"Look what came this morning," she panted as she met Agnes in the little lobby.

It was a picture postcard from Siôn in France addressed to Miss Elin Roberts, and there was a short standard message printed on it, to the effect that his unit had been pulled out of the line after the battle for Mametz Wood. As a result the two girls were jubilant, and my mother said:

"Perhaps he'll get some leave now and we'll see him."

But at the same time, she was wondering why Siôn had chosen to tell Elin such important news and not his own people.

She had very little opportunity to think about such details during the course of the next few days however. She took back Harriet's clothes and she was accorded the same kind of welcome, but that time she made sure of returning before dark, and as she crossed the Dead Marsh she could not help shuddering when she looked at the swinging bog where her unmarked grave could have been.

She also went to the vicarage in the Conwy Valley to terminate her engagement and she brought her box away with her. Then she went to see the old parson who, within the week, had arranged for her to go for an interview for the post of house-maid to an establishment in Anglesey called Plas Llwynhidil.

It was a very hot day when she crossed on the boat from Bangor to Beaumaris. She had a long way to walk again inland, and when she reached the main lodge by the archway that had written on it 'Welcome ye coming, speed ye parting guest', she was weary and thirsty.

When she pulled the bell chain, an old man ambled out of the lodge to open the gate for her. She showed him her letter, and by then an old lady had also come out, followed by a small girl. When they had established the purpose of my mother's errand, the old lady said,

"Come inside a minute out of the heat my maid." And to the child: "Get her a glass of butter-milk Lisi, and bring one for Tomos Puw while you're at it."

The lodge was cool and restful to Mother after the heat. She sat across the hearth from the old couple, and when the child brought the butter-milk she held it out as if she was serving at the altar. Then she stood in the middle of the floor gaping at Agnes.

"I heard you were coming to be house-maid," said the old lady. "You're from the other side, they say. How did you get across?"

She was quizzing faster than my mother could answer, until the old man said, "Don't delve in the girl's basket, Catrin."

She desisted for a moment, which gave Agnes a chance to look about her. The place had a more prosperous air than her home at Llan Isa. There was a row of photographs on the mantel, one she noticed of a young soldier with a Welch Fusilier badge on his cap. Agnes thought then that there would be no harm in asking a few questions herself.

"Who is that?"

"Our Harry," said the old man. "He's in France. We had a card from him — when was it — last week? Show it to her Catrin."

When the old lady brought the card, Agnes saw that it was

identical to the one that Siôn had sent Elin, and she said so with surprise.

"Well I never," said the old lady.

"They both must have been at Mametz," said Mother.

"Do you think so, girl?" The old lady sighed. "I get awfully anxious about him sometimes."

They were discussing that when the telephone rang. The old man go up laboriously to answer it, and Agnes heard him say:

"Yes, my lady. Very good, my lady."

"I shall have to go and open the gates," he said importantly. "Her Ladyship is going out. Come Lisi," he said to the child "to help me with the gravel." But the girl was not too anxious to go. She was much more interested in Agnes.

"Get on with you child," said the old lady, "standing there gawping."

As Agnes watched the child scuttling out, she could not but see shades of her own self at Faenol Grand Lodge, and she asked:

"Who is she then?"

"She's from the orphanage. Her Ladyship is one of the governors, you see. She got the girl here to start her off. She'll go to the big house later."

Presently they heard horses trotting by. "That's her now," said the old lady. "She's off to London for a fortnight. Nice for some."

"It must be," said Agnes. "But how will I see her now?"

"You won't have to my maid. Mc Kage the housekeeper deals with engagements. I don't want to turn you against her mind, but she can be an old badger."

"I see," said my mother, rather surprised that a woman so fond of questioning could be so revealing. "I'd better be footing it," and she stood to go. "Thank you for the butter-milk."

"Don't mention. We might be seeing more of you."

"No telling."

When she went out again on the drive, Tomos Puw and the little maid were raking the gravel back into the carriage tracks.

"I may as well be throwing my hat against the wind as do this," he said. "He'll be back again in a minute."

And so it proved. Agnes had not gone very far down the drive when she was overtaken by an open landau drawn by two black horses. The coachman on the box wore a high hat with a cockade, and behind sat two footmen with powdered wigs. The coachman reined in the horses, and he called down to Agnes:

"Where be you going to my pretty maid? Jump in and keep your head down."

The carriage rounded a bend, and my mother saw Llwynhidil for the first time. It looked wonderful she said, with its grey stone porticos and colonnades, and wide green lawns. And I can imagine that the sight would catch at the breath of a country girl, especially if she had prospects of living there.

The carriage swept round the corner of the big conservatory where the exotic flowers grew. She alighted, and the coachman doffed his hat with an exaggerated flourish, while one of the footmen told her where to go. She rang a bell at a large door, and presently a maid appeared. She led my mother inside to a bare office, and there she waited for some time in great suspense until eventually a tall woman, dressed severely all in black with a lorgnette hanging round her neck, arrived.

"You're Agnes Jones," she said without preamble. "Well stand girl, stand when you're spoken to, and if you ever have occasion to come here again, will you be good enough to use the other entrance?"

She then sat at a table, lifted the lorgnette, and told Agnes to walk to the door, turn about and come back. When she had done this, the woman said:

"I understand you wish to fill the post of second house-maid here. Your rector has already sent your character reference. Have you any more?"

Agnes produced a letter which she had from her last employer. The woman read parts of it aloud. "I see," she said at last. "You have not had any experience of the kind of work that will be required of you in an establishment of this kind. You will be working six and a half days a week. The day starts at six, and it goes on until six in the evening with one hour for lunch. You will receive twelve pounds per annum all found. You will attend church every Sunday morning, and you will be allowed beer money, and one free day per month. What say you?"

"All right, I suppose," said my mother, country-soft, having hardly had the time to take it all in.

"All right — Mrs Mc Kage," said the housekeeper. "You'll address me as such at all times, if you are engaged. Have you any questions?"

"Um — no," said my mother.

"Very well. If you are successful, you will be sent for." She rang a bell. "Good day," she said and swept out. The maid reappeared and showed Agnes out through another door without saying a word.

After that reception, Agnes did not hold out much hope of an engagement at the mansion in Anglesey, and she began to think of alternatives, but two Sundays after, in the church porch after Morning Prayer, the old parson drew her aside, and said that he'd had word about her from Llwynhidil. She was to start upon her duties there in two days' time.

It was such short notice, that she hardly had time to put her little affairs in order and pack her box, less still to say goodbye to Joss. She always maintained to the very end, that in spite of the long hours and the low wages, and the restrictions, her term as house-maid in Llwynhidil was a very happy time, and when one thinks about the social conditions of that era, a girl of her station could hardly have done better under the circumstances. She at least knew exactly where she stood, and she lived under the establishment's umbrella, inside a self-supporting unit. They depended on no one from the outside — apart from the local watchmaker who came once a week to wind all the clocks.

His Lordship was serving in the war, at sea, but the routine of the house and gardens and home-farm ran smoothly under the supervision of experts, overseen by the lady herself. She was a handsome woman of good carriage, my mother said, and she had the welfare of the servants always in mind. She had a grown-up son, an infantry officer commanding a battalion of local troops in France, and a daughter.

The establishment had hung on to modes and customs relinquished by others of its kind. The footmen still wore livery and powdered wigs. There was an annual servants' ball, and, as the housekeeper had already outlined, there was compulsory church attendance.

In the evenings, the girls would wander down to the bothies to banter with the old gardeners, and when guests came to dance, they were allowed to spectate from the gallery upon the activities below, and unconsciously they began to adopt the manner of their employers in speech, dress and behaviour, and they made comparisons with their own simple beginnings.

My mother shared duties with a lively and talkative girl from Ireland called Bridget. They were expected to look after two rooms on the second floor and keep them in daily order. They washed the small change, they ironed the morning papers before setting them out on the tables, and when they moved furniture for cleaning, they stuck pins in the carpets, so that the articles could be replaced in exactly the same positions.

Agnes sent a card with a photograph of the house and lawns to Joss, and she was eagerly looking forward to her free day on the mainland. In the meantime something singular happened that demolished her expectations.

Ellis Williams the gaucho

FIVE

She was upstairs with Bridget one after-noon, when the girl called her excitedly to the window,

"Come here Agnes. Who is this?"

When Mother went to her side, she saw a man in khaki coming up the drive with his arm in a sling.

"Siôn ... it's our Siôn," she shouted hastily, and she ran down the main stairway, completely ignoring the house rules, and across the hall. She flung open the front door and dashed across the lawn.

But she had occasion to pull up short. It wasn't her brother at all, but the boy from the lodge. When she made that discovery, she turned on her heel and walked back into the house crestfallen, only to be confronted at the door by the housekeeper.

"Go to my office at once," she said.

Agnes waited in the office for a long time, in even greater suspense than she had been the previous time. When the housekeeper appeared at last, she demanded,

"What is the meaning of this kind of behaviour?"

Agnes tried to explain her mistake as best she could, but Mrs. Mc Kage did not allow her to finish.

"That's as it may be, but you know very well what the house rules are. What are they?"

"Not to run, Mrs. Mc Kage."

"Very well. I shall report you to her Ladyship in the morning. In the meantime you will forfeit your next free day. Well, what have you to say?"

"Yes, Mrs Mc Kage."

"You may go."

When my mother returned upstairs, Bridget said:

"You got off very lightly, my girl. That's a very touchy thing with old Mac, running and skipping in the house. But what in the name of all the saints made you do it?"

"I thought he was my brother."

"Never mind Agi. He'll come you'll see; he'll come."

But the day was not without its compensations. In the evening Agnes went down to the lodge to see the old couple. And she saw their son, this time properly. He assured her that he had seen Siôn in France, and that he was well. Later he accompanied her up the drive, and she had an opportunity to ask him more questions.

A piece of shrapnel had shattered his elbow, and he expected to go to a military hospital for treatment. Because of this it was very unlikely that he would be sent back to France. He had 'copped a Blighty' as he put it, and Agnes was astounded to hear him say, that the wish of the majority was to 'cop a Blighty' so that they could be sent home. He even knew of one or two who had injured themselves deliberately.

"What was it like?" she asked innocently, but he pretended not to hear, and he assured her again that he had seen Siôn one moon-light, when their battalion was coming down from the line and his was going up near Mametz.

In the morning Mrs. Mc Kage sent for Agnes. "You're to come with me to see her Ladyship," she said. "And remember, you're not to speak until you're spoken to."

Agnes followed her upstairs. The lady was in her room, writing at her desk, and she did not raise her head for a minute. When she did at last, she also did a singular thing. She asked the housekeeper to leave. Agnes was not prepared for her first question.

"Are you happy here Agnes?"

"Yes, my lady."

"Why then did you break the rules of the house, er — yesterday was it?"

"Well ..." my mother began, but the lady helped her.

"You thought that your brother had come?"

"Yes, my lady."

"You think quite a lot of your brother I understand, and you've only just lost another?"

My mother didn't know what to say. Apparently her case history had arrived before her. But the lady went on.

"But that does not mean that you can break the house rules does it?"

"No, my lady."

"Where is your brother, Agnes?"

"In France, my lady. On the Somme somewhere. Mametz they say."

The lady looked for a moment at the far wall, as if she was trying to convey herself to places far away.

"It's an uncertain time for us all Agnes," she said. "Very uncertain." She put down her pen. "My son is in that area too, commanding a battalion. When did you last see your brother?"

"About a year ago."

The lady sighed. "As much as that? Do you remember his rank and number?"

Those details were stamped indelibly on my mother's mind, and she recited them like the Apostles' Creed.

"As it happens, I'm writing to Charles today," the lady went on, picking up her pen. "Goodness knows when he'll get it, but we'll see what we can do." She smiled. "There we are then. You may go."

Agnes turned about and was walking away, when the lady spoke again. "And Agnes — no more running across the house to meet strangers."

"No, my lady."

In a little over a fortnight, my mother received a postcard from Dover. It was from Siôn and he was coming home on leave.

Agnes shared a room with Bridget at the top of the house, and the night before she was going home to see Siôn, she was too excited to sleep. In the morning she was ready with the dawn breezes. Downstairs she had to pass Mrs. Mc Kage's inspection: she was sent back to re-do her hair, and as a result she very nearly missed the boat at the landing.

It was a beautiful morning as she climbed the hill from Felinheli station. (The weather was always nice in my mother's stories). When she got to the flat bit between Boncan Sipsiwn and Cefn Gwyn Farm, she saw a soldier with a full pack and a slung rifle coming to meet her. It was such a common sight in those days, that Agnes did not realise at first that it was her own brother, but when she did, she dropped her bundle on the road and ran to meet him. She threw herself on his neck, and neither could say a word. Siôn at last pushed her away at arm's length, and looked at her as if she was newly risen from the sea, and my mother was naïve enough to think that he had come on one purpose — to meet her. Instead of that, when he had a chance to explain, he told her he was on his way back to the trenches. He had received a telegram to cut short his leave, and he did not have much time to spare until his train went either.

Agnes went back with him, arm in arm, and she had his rifle slung on her shoulder. From time to time, she glanced at his profile slyly. She saw that he was gaunt and worn, looking tired and old before his time, and his eyes were still. He did not have much to say either, and when Agnes asked him what kind of a place it was in France, he pretended, like the boy at the lodge, not to have heard. Instead he took out his bayonet and cut a sprig of young broom for her off the hedge, and she kept that for years between the pages of 'The Travels of Livingstone'.

But she pressed him to tell her what had happened at home, and he said that my grand-father had stayed away from work for a day, that they had gone to town with Ruth, and on the Aber pleasure-boat. He had been to Rynys Lwyd to see Mari Lewis, and in Pen Rhyd, one after-noon he had gone with Elin to Tomos Morus's shop, and on the Old Celtic Fort to look down on Gors Farm and Arthur's Well; and Elin had told him about Joss, and taken a bit too much on herself in my mother's estimation. He had brought with him three fleur-de-lys brooches for the girls, and he had left my mother's on the glass cupboard shelf, but he mentioned nothing about Rolant until he had to.

"I didn't know until I met Gwen Fachall on the road when I was coming home, and she offered her condolences."

"But I wrote to tell you," said Agnes.

"I was in the line for three months, girl."

He would not let her go with him to the station on any account. He was determined to go on his own, and she had to be satisfied with standing in the middle of the road, watching him go. He did not once look back. She said that there were shafts of sun-light coming through the hazels on the bank, and as he moved from light to shade, she saw him as a ghost already; she knew that his time was going to be short.

She very nearly went straight back to Beaumaris then, but on she went, home to Llan Isa, and on the way she could only see Siôn's eyes in front of her; June sky eyes as she called them.

When she reached the house, Elin was in the living kitchen, in her Sunday best, and she had been crying. But she soon recovered when Agnes had told her that she had seen Siôn.

"He was dying to come and see you," said Elin, "only he thought he might do you harm at your new place. What did you think of him? I very nearly went with him to Felinheli for company, only I was afraid someone might see me, and I would be the talk of the whole parish."

"Why are you such a swell on a workday Elin?"

"I was going to tell you," said Elin, now restored to her exuberant self. "Aunty Grace came yesterday from Bethesda. She's full of rheumatics, and I'm going to take her to Ffynnon Arthur for the water. She's keen on going, and Bob Mul is going to take us in the round cart this after-noon. Why don't you come with us?"

"I can't. I want to see father and Ruth."

"We'll be back by quarry supper. Come on. We'll have some fun. I'll bring the boiling can and the bread-and-butter."

Agnes was persuaded by that. Within the hour she was waiting for Bob Mul by the road gate. He had never been short with his favours, but he was not keen upon going as far as Arthur's Well in such heat, and he didn't have much faith in the healing properties of the water either, at least not as far as Elin's aunt was concerned. "We may as well duck her in Tan Dinas pond," he said, "and save ourselves the journey." But on they went to Pen Rhyd to pick the old lady up. Then they laboured up Caerau Hill, and Bob was whipping at a cloud of flies with a frond.

There were people living in the house at Arthur's Well then, and there was a hut in the garden, used as a changing room, and in addition to the well itself, there were several rectangular slate baths on the bank of the Cegin river, where the invalids were immersed. It was a miniature Lourdes in the middle of the marshes, without the trappings.

Elin's Aunty Grace was slim of nature and tendency, and by the time the girls got her stripped, and into her night gown, they had to keep her facing front on, to assure themselves that there was anything left of her. Bob was wise enough to keep out of the way, but he had a chance to whisper once to my mother:

"When you put her in the water, she'll float like a stick. The shock of it will be enough to send her one way or the other I should think."

And by the time they got her in the water, Agnes began to wonder whether Bob Mul was not right after all. The old aunt began to snatch her breath, and she couldn't see herself being lifted out soon enough to get back to sit by her fire in Bethesda.

Bob had by then lit a wood fire by the rock pool to boil the billy, and when Agnes came to see how things were shaping, he said,

"I'm sure that old girl was a good singer in her time."

"What makes you think that?" asked my mother.

"She's got legs like a canary."

When Elin brought her aunt to join them, the water was boiling and the tea was on the go. Agnes was doling out the bread, and she didn't dare look at Bob Mul, but his attitude soon changed when the old lady said at last,

"You're very kind to bring us all this way, Mr Roberts."

She ingratiated herself still further by praising the tea, and saying how nice it tasted out-of-doors in such jolly company. When she asked Bob why he had put a little twig of oak in the billy can, and he had gone to the trouble of explaining that it was to prevent the water taking on the taste of smoke, they plunged into a conversation about the long ago time and the state of things generally; and when it transpired that Bob's cousin twice removed was now living next-door-but-one to the old aunt at Bethesda, and what a small world it was after all said and done, they were in a deep tête-à-tête which allowed the girls to follow their own devices.

They went to the top of the rock from where they could see half the parish, but Siôn was not far from their minds.

"I wonder where he is now?" said one.

"I wonder ..."

Then they saw some men haymaking in Bifan field.

"That's Joss, the tall one with the pikle," said Elin. "Are you going to take him a cup of tea?"

"Sh...sh," whispered Agnes, for she knew that if Bob Mul overheard, her life would not be worth living for the rest of the after-noon.

Elin then sat on the step at the bottom of the rock, bathing her feet.

"Look at that big eel!" Bob shouted.

"Where, where?" screamed Elin, and she jumped into a gorse-bush, (and my mother spent the rest of the after-noon taking the prickles out of her soles). Just then they heard the quarrymen's train hooting, across the meadows.

"Goodness, is it all that time already?" asked Agnes. "I was supposed to be home to make the quarry supper. My father will have something to say."

SIX

She was right about her father. He was in a temper.

"Where have you been, moidering all day with that girl?" he asked.

It appeared that he had promised to go and help Mari Lewis with the haymaking, and Ruth had been sent home from school because she wasn't well.

"Why didn't you come to see Siôn?" asked her father again.

But he calmed down when Mother told him that she had seen Siôn after all, and how the Lady of Llwynhidil had been instrumental in getting him leave in the first place. Then they began to exchange observations about Siôn.

"I thought that he had aged in a short time," said my grand-father. "And he had a mean look about him, he didn't have much to say either. He did nothing but walk the fields with the dog and follow Elin everywhere. He was with that girl every minute. I told him too. I don't know what Dafydd Fachall would have to say."

Agnes however, did not let on that she had not gone to the station with her brother, and then they began to exchange the day's news.

"There was a story going in the quarry today that Robin Duff, the squire's brother, has had the silver bullet in France."

"What's that?" asked Ruth.

"Getting shot by his own men of course. It was only to be expected so they say, the way he was treating them."

"There's one thing for certain," said Agnes. "Our Siôn didn't do it. He wasn't there."

In the evening, Bob Mul came again with his turn out to take Aunty Grace to the train and Agnes went with them. She was not by then quite so anxious about her father and Ruth. She knew that Elin was in and out every day, keeping an eye on them, so as she went for the boat by the pier she thought of other things: of how she had been so near to Joss that after–noon an yet so far, she would have to wait for another month; and she wondered if she would ever see Siôn again, and where was he now?

As she was walking from the landing at the other side, she heard her name called.

"Miss Jones, are you going home?"

When she turned, she saw Harry Puw the lodge. He was in mufti, and if it hadn't been for the sling on his arm, she would not have recognised him.

"I'm going too," he said. "Can I walk with you?"

They went in silence for a while, and then the boy said,

"Did you have a nice day on the other side? Did you see Siôn?"

"Yes," said Mother in answer to both questions, "but he had been recalled you see, before his leave was over."

"That's what they always do when they've got a big push in mind."

He might have thought that he had spoken out of turn, for he stopped talking all of a sudden, but presently he blurted,

"They've spoilt me anyway. They've spoilt me for ever."

"You musn't think like that," said Mother. "Those doctors are very clever now you know."

"They think they are, anyway," he said, his voice breaking, and when Agnes glanced side-ways at him, she saw that he was crying. They had gone beyond Llanfaes and were walking between the high green hedges.

She let him recover, and then he said, "I'm sorry, Miss Jones, but it's hard not to sometimes, although I'm not ashamed with you somehow."

"I don't mind," said Mother.

"It's not so much getting back to my work in the garden you see, but I had other hopes, and they've been dashed."

Agnes immediately thought that he had plans of marrying or something like that. She said nothing; neither did he. But like the cat, her curiosity overcame her.

"What had you planned to do then?" she asked.

"Draw," he said emphatically.

"Draw? Oh you mean — draw pictures like?"

"Yes, that's right. Do you think it's a silly thing for a man to be doing?"

"Not a bit. I wish I could draw. Are you good?"

"I used to be quite good at school. Of course I haven't had a chance to practise lately — you know."

"Yes. But what did you draw?"

"Nature things. Wild birds and that. I used to go down to the lake in the Park you see. There are all kinds of water-birds there. Have you ever been?"

"No," said Mother. "I knew there was a lake down there somewhere."

"Would — would you like to go one evening?"

"Well, yes if you like."

"Righto then. I've got some drawings in the house too. Would you like to see them?"

"Yes, but it's too late tonight."

"Another time then?"

"Yes, another time."

They had reached the lodge where the old couple were sitting on the porch enjoying the last light, and the little girl was playing with a wooden doll on the steps.

"*Duwcs,* I thought for a minute that you had found a sweetheart," said the old lady.

"I happened to bump into Miss Jones coming off the boat," said Harry.

"Get away. I've never known you have any interest in boats before."

Harry insisted upon coming with Agnes half-way up the drive, and before he left her, he had made another admission. The old couple were his grandparents. His parents had died when he was very young. After Mother had assimilated that fact, they made arrangements to go one evening to the lake in the Park.

Agnes had to report her arrival to Mrs. Mc Kage. The housekeeper nodded and asked her if she'd had a nice day, and in doing so, automatically revealed that her own had not been so bad. She handed my mother a missive from the letter rack.

She went upstairs staring at the envelope all the way and pondering who it could be from. People did not rush to open letters then. They preferred to postpone the pleasure or the pain by studying the postmark and the date. Mother's letter had the Llanrug mark and a halfpenny stamp.

When she opened the door of her room, there was Bridget pirouetting in front of a mirror, in a long dress, and she was singing too.

"You sound happy," said Agnes. "What's the matter?"

"The coachman has asked me if he can take me to the servants' ball. But what have you got to say? How went your day? Well come on, tell."

Agnes did not know where to start, and she was dying to open her letter. She went to the window at last and ripped the envelope. Then she forgot everything else.

'My dear Agnes,' she read. The writing was laborious but legible. 'I was thinking about you today. I saw a lot of people at Arthur's Well, and I thought how nice it would be to sit by the Rock Pool with you. I am driving cattle to Anglesey on Tuesday. I shall be coming to Beaumaris for the boat in the evening. Try and come to the landing, your sweetheart, Joss.'

When Agnes turned to face Bridget again, her whole expression must have told a story.

"Good news is it?" asked the girl. "Is it still loving you he is, dear Agi?"

"Who?" asked Mother foolishly.

"Come away with you. It's bound to out sometime. I saw you coming home with Harry too."

"I happened to see him at the landing."

"And is that so now?"

"It's a shame for him, don't you think?"

"It is that," said the girl from County Clare, "but beware of pity girl, beware."

Agnes put on her best coat and bonnet to go and meet Joss in Beaumaris. When she was going past the lodge, she saw Harry standing at the gates.

"Are you going a walk, Miss Jones?" he asked.

"I'm going to town."

"I've a mind to go there too." And he must have assumed that Mother did not mind being accompanied. He walked by her side, but the atmosphere was not so relaxed as before, Agnes was trying to devise some excuse to be rid of him, but she was very conscious at the same time, she said, that she would not have to wound.

The boy seemed happy, and cheerful which made it much more difficult for my mother. In this manner they arrived at the water's edge, and there was Joss, with his cattle dog, waiting, and as soon as he saw her, he put up his hand, and came towards them. Harry was looking at Agnes and at the approaching figure by turn.

"I meant to say before," said Agnes at last. "I meant to say
... I was meeting someone."

"So I see," said Harry, and he went his own way.

Joss was pleased to see her, but he was inquisitive about
Harry. Agnes answered him casually, and she said,

"He's been very unlucky you know."

"He's still alive anyway," said Joss.

They walked slowly towards the landing. It was much too
public to allow them to demonstrate their affection. They had to
confine themselves to talking about their own simple rural
affairs. They watched the boat approaching from the other side,
and it seemed to arrive much too soon.

"You're very pretty tonight Agnes," said the boy. "June
blue eyes. When shall we have time together on the other side?"

"Next time," said my mother. "Next time," and she stood
by the landing watching the boat until it arrived at the other side.
She lingered for a long time, looking at the far shore.

But for all the anticipation and hope, Agnes did not see Joss
that next time. When she arrived home on her free day she
was surprised to find that there was hardly any food left in the
house, so she had to spend most of the day fetching some.
When my grand-father arrived from the quarry, almost the first
thing she said was:

"You seem to be getting through an awful lot of food these
days."

"Are we? I hadn't noticed girl. Elin looks after things like
that for us."

My mother did not give the matter much thought, that is
until Mari Lewis came later and said during the conversation,

"I don't know if it's me getting old, but I've missed a *stên* of
butter-mild from the milk-house the other night."

"Things seem to be going to ruin everywhere Mari," said my
grand-father. "I heard a man on the train saying that someone
had broken into Tomos Morus's shop."

One evening that week, Agnes went with Harry Puw to the
lake shore in the Park, and he brought some of his drawings to
show her. He had not exaggerated one bit, she said, when he
claimed he could draw; the birds were as if they were actually
flying across the paper.

But she never let on to me how often they went to the lake. It
was a wonderful spot then apparently, and quiet. There was a
rowing-boat too, and she went out in that with Harry once or

twice, although she hated water.

Harry evicently enjoyed her company, and he was always curious about her relationship with Joss, and at times he could not conceal his jealousy.

"It's all right for the likes of him," he said once, "working on the land, well out of it. There are dozens of his kind in Anglesey here too."

But Agnes wouldn't have him misunderstand the situation at any price.

"Joss's brother has been killed you know," she bridled. "After coming all the way from Australia too."

"What was he doing there?" asked Harry.

Then mother went through all the case history, as if she was being paid for being defending counsel.

"He was sent away for poaching and he became a *gaucho* in Patagonia, and to escape conscription into the Argentine army he went to Australia, and he had a sheep-farm..." And she only desisted when Harry, now suitably impressed, said,

"And he left all that to come to France and get killed?"

One particular evening they had stayed over-long at the lake. Harry had been lamenting the fact that he could not possibly train himself to draw with his left hand, that his genius only flowed down his other arm. They were returning along the rhododendron walk in the twilight, when the little child Lisi ran to meet them full of agitation.

"Miss Jones, Miss Jones," she panted. "Come quickly, there's a man at the gates that wants to see you."

When Mother and Harry arrived at the lodge, they saw Joss standing by the main gates. He came forward and grabbed Agnes by the arm.

"Agnes, I want to see you," he said without preamble, and he took no notice at all of her companion. She was put out by his manner, and annoyed, but when she was at last persuaded to go with him into the road, her annoyance drained away.

"Listen Agnes," said Joss. "Siôn is at our house."

SEVEN

After receiving that astounding piece of news, Agnes did not know what to do, but her actions were decided for her, as they were then for most people. She could do very little about anything until her next free day, neither could she confide in anyone. Joss had only time to tell her that he had found Siôn in the barn one morning, cold and hungry and bearded like a *poilu*, but most of all he had stressed that she was not to tell anyone; not even her father and Ruth.

At any rate, she was glad that Siôn was alive, but the poor girl had not then considered the seriousness of the situation. She was glad of Harry's company during those weeks when they went to the lake side in the evenings. He evidently enjoyed her company too. Once or twice she was on the point of telling him about Siôn.

When her free day at last arrived, she was confused and apprehensive. She did not go home. She went the roundabout way to Gors Farm, even avoiding Pen Rhyd. Even so, she thought that everybody was watching her. Siôn was very pleased to see her, but she noticed that he was ashamed too. He looked a lot better. He was evidently well-fed and he did some odd work about the steading and kept out of sight. Joss had buried his equipment in the Dead Marsh and had lit a fire over the spot.

When Agnes asked him what he had been doing and where he had been since he was on the run, Siôn was evasive and vague, and she could get very little out of him. "I just kept out of sight you know," he said. But after seeing him, Agnes felt better. She was hard put however to conceal her feelings from her father and Ruth later in the day, because the first thing she was asked was:

"Have you heard from Siôn?"

"No," she said with some truth. "Have you?"

"Do you think he's been killed like Rolant?" Ruth asked.

"No, he's all right you'll see," said Agnes. "The post takes a long time to come from France. I went to Gors today to see how they were. Anne Jane Williams has asked me to go to Glasgoed chapel next month to Ellis's memorial service."

"Oh has she?" said her father. "Just as well you went then. You're getting friendly with Anne Jane. Next thing I suppose you'll be marrying that boy Joss?"

"I don't know indeed," said my mother. "There are a lot of things likely to happen before that."

"Like what then?" Ruth asked.

Agnes was glad of another tack to lead the conversation away from Siôn, and she said:

"The servants' ball for one thing."

Ruth was anxious to know more about that.

"Well, we dress in our best you see," said Agnes. "I shall have to get a long gown from somewhere. Then we go to the main hall to eat, and then we dance, and everybody takes a partner."

"Who will be your partner then?"

"I don't know yet, but I'm bound to get someone."

"Can't you take Joss?"

"No. It has to be someone on the premises."

"What will *he* say?"

"Oh nothing I expect." The little girl was getting too persistent Mother thought, so she said: "But the best thing is, it's the people themselves who will be waiting on us that night."

"The Lady herself?" asked Ruth, and her eyes were like saucers.

"Oh yes, that's the custom," said Mother importantly, as if she had taken part in it for half a century.

There was a thunder-storm on the night that Agnes went to Ellis Williams's memorial service in Glasgoed chapel. She sat with the family in the Gors pew, between Harriet and Anne Jane. The thunder was so deafening she said, that on occasions they could hardly hear the preacher, and Agnes was fighting her emotions when she thought of Siôn hiding in the cave he had in the big rick in the barn at Gors. To end the service they sang, 'Lead us into pastures verdant' to the tune of 'Austria', and they lifted it to the beams, little realising that it was the national anthem of the people who had brought so much sorrow into their lives. The congregation filed out into the lightning — riven darkness, and Agnes went to supper with the Gors family, together with Harriet's husband-to-be, thereby making a public

46

sign that she eventually had intentions of becoming a member herself.

She bade farewell to Siôn at the supper table, and Joss escorted her all the way home, as the iron water of Arthur's Well drew the lightning like kitchen forks into the marshes.

The months went by one by one, and everyone was hoping for a Christmas of peace, but it was not to be. Agnes went regularly to see the Gors family, and it seemed so natural, because everyone in the parish knew that Joss and she were courting.

But one free day, Elin was waiting for her by the pump, and she had disturbing news. She said that two soldiers with red caps had been to Llan Isa looking for Siôn. There was only Ruth at home, and Mother was thanking God by then, that the girl knew nothing about Siôn. The soldiers had been to Pen Rhyd, and Rynys Lwyd, and they had been in the churchyard too, said Elin. After that, everyone knew that something had happened to Siôn.

During the course of that week it was the night of the servants' ball at Llwynhidil. Agnes by then had little enthusiasm. It was a bright moon-light night, and Harry Puw asked her at the last minute if he could accompany her. The hall had been decorated, the tables set, and everyone was wearing his best. Present too were Charles, the son who was home that week on leave, and his sister from the West Country. Agnes had not seen either of them before. Charles was in his uniform, looking smart; all the girls were eyeing him, and Agnes thought that he had a slight limp.

After the feast, the dancing began, and Harry with his bad arm, was no great shakes at leading Mother across the floor. She detatched herself and sat on her own for a moment to watch the others. She had not been seated many moments when Charles came up to her and introduced himself politely. He, in his turn, had not seen her before, but apparently, he had been told who she was.

"You are Siôn Rowland Jones's sister aren't you?" he said.

"Yes."

"How is he?" he asked suddenly.

"I don't know," said Mother, and she felt her face warming, but she faced him and added, "He hasn't written for some time."

The man said no more about it, but he spoke again,

"Could I see you privately in my room?"

She was at a loss what to say. She had heard so much about

girls being lured by men like that, and 'getting into trouble' as the saying went, but the invitation seemed to be in the form of a command as well.

When she was admitted into the man's room, he was sitting at his desk, cigarette smoke ascending from his fist, and before she had time to compose herself, he asked her outright,

"Do you know anything about the whereabouts of your brother?"

But she stoutly denied any such knowledge, and the man did not press her, he merely said,

"The fact is that your brother is missing. He did not report to his unit when his leave expired."

"Is he dead?" whispered Agnes, and there was no need for her to pretend to be frightened.

"Worse that that, Agnes," Charles said. "He's run away. Deserted. Do you know what the penalty for that is?"

"No, I don't." And this time she was telling the truth.

He rose, walked towards the fireplace and threw his cigarette into the flames. By then, Agnes was certain that he was limping.

"Deserters face the firing squad at dawn, and it goes very hard against those who give them shelter as well — life imprisonment usually. Will you remember that, Agnes?"

She'd shrunk into herself, but she managed to say,

"Yes sir."

Charles went back to his seat and he lit another cigarette, and they said nothing for a while. Charles spoke first, and what he said astounded Agnes.

"But he has a great deal more guts than I have."

"How is that sir?"

He raised his voice. "Did he ever tell you what kind of a place it is? Did he?"

"No sir."

"It's a living hell on earth Agnes; blood, mud and corpses. I shall be back amongst it within the week. Your brother and his kind have more sense keeping well clear of it."

There was another unpleasant silence.

"Have you been hurt?" asked Agnes in a minute.

"A bullet graze in my leg. It's nothing."

He stood up then and extended his hand to my mother. "Good luck Agnes," he said. "You'd better get back to the ball. Harry will miss you. He needs someone to look after him."

After that meeting with Charles, Agnes found it difficult to set her mind to anything. She had to tell *someone,* she had to, before the suspense became too much for her. It had to be Harry or Bridget. Elin she had decided was much too near home.

It was a custom at Llwynhidil for the maids to get up at crack of dawn, taking turns accompanying the coachmen to exercise the horses. Agnes and Bridget went one morning as far as Penmon Priory. On the way back in the landau, when the sun was just starting to glint on the Straits, and to the sound of the horses' hooves, Agnes poured out all her troubles to Bridget; but to her surprise, the Irish girl turned not a hair. Her brother too was on the run in his own country, she said, after the Easter Rising.

"I'll take Siôn across the water the next time I go," she said. "My people will look after him."

And from that day a bond was tied between Agnes and Bridget that only death in the end tore apart.

But had they only known it, that was only the beginning of an eventful day. When they got back from the stables, Mrs. Mc Kage summoned them to her office. She had a grimmer mien than usual.

"We've had bad new, I'm afraid," she said slowly. "Something I'm sure that will sadden us all. This morning, one of the keepers found young Harry Puw drowned in the Park Lake."

"Drowned!" exclaimed my mother, and sat down without permission.

"Yes," said the housekeeper. "He was underneath the capsized boat it seems. His drawings were scattered all over the water." She paused for a while. "That will be all. Will you carry on with your duties in the quietest manner possible?"

The two girls went slowly up the great staircase arm in arm. They reached the landing, and then they threw themselves on the banister rail, sobbing.

The servants who could be spared from the duties of the day went to Harry's funeral. They filed by the graveside, and Mother and Bridget each threw a wayside flower upon the coffin. In the evening Agnes went down to the lodge. The old couple's world had come apart, and for the time being the Lady had arranged for them to be relieved of their duties. There was not much that Agnes could say to them. The old lady kept repeating over and over:

"We thought that he would be safe after having done with that old war. But he died at home in the end."

And to herself Agnes kept repeating: "There will be no boys left."

Ellis Williams, the soldier.

EIGHT

Thanksgiving time came along then, and Agnes spent the best part of one free day, decorating the Old Church with Elin, and Mari Lewis brought her annual sheaf of corn, insisting as usual, that it should be hung on the pulpit side, so that it could be seen by all the congregation.

And before Christmas came the wedding-day of Elin and Dafydd. My mother was the bridesmaid, and she had prepared a dinner for them at Llan Isa. Bob Mul was there too, to take them to the train, and Jini Wen's bridle and the round cart were festooned with ribbons. Mari Lewis was there, offering wisdom and dispensing advice; a bit too late for Elin, Agnes thought. It was obvious that she was carrying someone else's burden, and she didn't seem to be a happy bride at all.

By then, Agnes was used to the idea of Siôn being at Gors. The red-caps did not reappear, and Anne Jane Williams was getting fond of Siôn; but it was all a fool's paradise. When Agnes came home one cold morning in January, with the East wind whistling through Tan Dinas woods, she saw a white cloth hanging out of Pen Rhyd bedroom window; a sign that she was required there in a hurry.

She threw her things on the table and rushed out through the gate, but she'd hardly got further than the pump, when Elin came to meet her at a run. She grabbed my mother round the neck and started sobbing.

"Well what's the matter Elin? Why are you breaking your heart like this?"

"Siôn has been killed," cried Elin over and over. "He's been kicked by a horse…"

"Kicked… killed… Siôn?" My mother released Elin and she went and hung on to the stem of the pump for dear life. "But why Elin? Why? He was so safe. He wasn't in the war. Why Elin?"

"I don't know Agnes. I don't know. But it was my fault. He would have been alive but for me."

Agnes let go the pump and she took hold of Elin's arm.

"But for you? What do you mean?"

"I sent him there. I sent him to Gors to begin with."

"You? Come my dear. We'll go in the house. You can tell me there." But Elin could not restrain herself as they went arm in arm towards the house, she kept repeating:

"It was my fault."

When they got to the house, Agnes sat across the fire to Elin, and then she realised that the girl had another problem not so far distant. Her child was due in a couple of months. She decided to allow her to tell her story in her own time.

Elin began to relate with relief and passion, but my mother was so eager for the facts that she didn't know what she wanted to be told first.

"Where's my father and Ruth?" she asked.

"They don't know yet," said Elin.

"When was he killed then?"

"Yesterday."

"And you didn't tell my father?"

"I didn't know what to do for best. I wanted to see you first."

"Why?"

"It was only me and the Gors family who knew about Siôn."

"How did *you* know then?"

"I came across him one evening in the dusk. I'd gone to see Mari Lewis, and I heard someone in the milk-house. I went there thinking it was her, and there he was."

"What did you do then?"

"I went with him to Tan Dinas woods," she said at last, and she was hanging her head. "That's where he lived you see, and on the Old Fort; that is until it got to be too cold. Then he had to go indoors somewhere. I told him to go to the hay barn in Gors. If he was caught there, they would be the least likely to snitch. And I was right, wasn't I?" she insisted, to justify herself.

"Yes, you were," said Agnes. "But I knew too, you know."

"I should have tumbled that, and you going there so often. Why didn't you say then, girl?"

"Well there you are. Why didn't you?"

"Siôn had made me promise not to, believe me, in case we were all drawn into trouble."

"But you knew that I was going there all the time."

"I tell you I promised, and I was afraid too."

"Yes, I know. It doesn't matter. I understand now why the food was getting low all the time. You were feeding him as well."

"Don't blame me for that Agnes. I'd never steal for anyone else. You would have done it yourself if you were in my situation. I thought the world of him you see. It was him I wanted but ..."

She began to sob.

"Calm your soul, Elin *bach*," said Mother, putting her hand on the girl's thigh. "It wasn't your fault, not any of it. But tell me one thing. Did you have anything to do with breaking into Tomos Morus's shop?"

"Well I didn't do it, but I went to keep a look out."

"It was Siôn then?"

"Yes, yes, he did it, but he was starving girl, don't forget — starving." She was shouting.

My mother realised then that there was nothing to be gained by subjecting Elin to remorse. It was obvious that love and loyalty had made her into a thief. But it did not matter to Agnes at the time; she knew that she had far worse things to face before the day was done. She had to go to Gors, and she tried to persuade Elin not to come, but to no avail. As things turned out however, she was glad of her company.

For the second time that year, Agnes looked down on a dead brother. The Gors family had taken Siôn to the front room, and Anne Jane Williams was taking his death as a personal responsibility, because she, under the old yeoman rules was still the head of the family. Agnes had always imagined Siôn being killed in France, and being 'thrown into a hole' as Joss had said, but here he was, killed within a mile of his own home after trying so hard to stay alive. And how uncommon was the situation. Even his death had to be concealed. It was all so contrary to the rural custom. There would be no one coming to offer condolences or help of any kind. She even detected some reticence to talk about the funeral arrangements.

When everyone was congregated in the living kitchen, Agnes asked at last,

"When are we going to have the funeral?"

It was a question that had to come, they all knew, but when it was finally asked, they were struck dumb, but in the end Anne Jane said,

"It's not so easy as that you see girl."

Then Agnes suddenly remembered the night of the servants' ball at Llwynhidil, and what Charles had said,

"It will go hard against anyone sheltering..."

"What shall we do, then?" she asked.

Everyone knew the answer, but no one was prepared to utter it. They were all looking at Anne Jane. She in turn was looking directly at Agnes.

"Put him in the Dead Marsh in the night," she said.

Agnes shot to her feet. "The Dead Marsh!" she shouted. "No indeed you won't! I'll tell my father," she said like a child being bullied at school. "He'll know what to do. Come Elin. We'll go." And she even refused Joss's offer to send them across the marshes.

When my mother got home, she didn't know how to tell her father and Ruth about Siôn, but tell them she had to, and they were both prostrated, especially when they realised that Siôn could not be buried publicly.

After recovering, my grand-father said, "I'll go and see them tonight. You go back to your place like a brave girl as if nothing has happened. I'll send you a message in the morning."

And she had to go and leave everything. She and Bridget were awake all night discussing all the possibilities, but they could devise no better a solution for the problem.

About noon the following day, Bob Mul came with the round cart to look for Agnes.

"They've found your brother at last, little girl," he said.

"Found him?" asked Agnes in wonder and fear. "What do you mean?"

"First thing this morning at Arthur's Well by the slate baths. He'd struck his head on the edge of one they say." He paused. "He's — dead you know."

"But Bob..." Agnes commenced, but she had the sense to pull up short when she realised that he knew nothing about Siôn. She went to see Mrs. Mc Kage who gave her permission to go home, and she offered condolences. But on the way she was a puzzled girl, and not very much was said. Bob said once, "To think that it wasn't so long ago that we were there — so happy."

Agnes ran into the house when they arrived, leaving Bob by the gate, and her father was there, in his high armchair, and in his Sunday best, just as he had been when Rolant was killed.

"What's the matter father?" she asked first thing. "What's happened to Siôn? Bob was saying..."

"Yes, yes I know," he said quietly. "Calm yourself girl. I'll tell you. I went to Gors last night, and I had a welcome. You would have thought that it was their own son, but I could see their difficulty, and it would be bad for us all if the truth ever came out, don't forget. After all you couldn't expect the people to put themselves in the path of punishment after they had sheltered him for so long."

"But why was he at Ffynnon Cegin Arthur?"

"Listen now. They had been discussing before I arrived, and Joss said that he was going to take Siôn on his back and leave him by the baths at the Well in the dark. Somebody would be bound to discover him in the morning. And that's what happened you see. The constable has been here, and no one is any the wiser so far. Of course, those old soldiers are bound to come. But they all think that he fell in the dark and struck his head you see."

"That means he will be buried in the churchyard?"

"Yes, thank God. And Joss is looking after all the arrangements for us. You've come across a good one there Agnes."

"Do you think so, father?"

It was a peculiar funeral that Siôn had at the Old Church. There was only the hearse, and the horses were without plumes, a handful of people, and few came to the house at all. There was no sending money, and the red capped soldiers were there, making sure that he was lowered the wrong way round as a sign of shame. Ruth was hanging on to my mother for dear life. Elin was there, heavy and unsteady, in the little hat she'd bought to bury Rolant, and she was breaking her heart. The old parson's Adam's apple was bobbing under his collar as he tried to persuade them that they would see Siôn again beyond some border, far away, but they were not convinced.

But as my mother said so many times, there were also the good chapters.

In the Spring, a son was born to Elin, and Agnes did not see the child until her first free day. Elin was waiting for her by the pump. She had the child in a shawl, and pinned to that, Agnes noticed, was the fleur-de-lys brooch. When they went into the house, Elin asked,

"Well, do you like him?"

"Oh, I do," said Agnes with envy. "What's he called then?"

"Siôn."

"Oh? Nice. June sky eyes too — like, like Rolant."

"And his brother," said Elin quietly.

"What?" said Agnes. "You don't mean to...?"

"He's a nearer relation than you think." Elin was smiling.

"Elin, *fach*, give him to me," said my mother. She took the child, and whipped the shawl round her shoulder. She walked slowly out into the garden, and there she stayed for a long time, nursing; the tears slipping down her cheeks.

But that was not the end of my mother's happy day. In the dusk, when she was setting out for the train at Felinheli, she saw someone standing by the pump. It was Joss in his cord breeches and his leggings hard polished.

"Where will you go at this hour?" asked my mother.

"To look for a wife," he said. "Do you know of one?"

"I don't," she said. "What would you be doing with one anyway?"

"I'm going to buy a farm, and I would want her to come and live there with me."

"Anybody would think that you were serious."

"They'd be right. Come here. I want to tell you something."

"I haven't got much time. I'm late for the train."

"Never mind that. You might not have to go on it much longer."

"Oh? How's that?"

"Listen Agnes," the boy said, putting his hand on the dome of the pump. "I've had a letter from Australia. Those old solicitors have sorted out Ellis's affairs at last. I've had all his property."

"You? But if you marry and go away, what will become of your mother and sister?"

"Harriet is marrying too. Her husband is coming to live at home."

My mother was too astonished to say anything by then.

"And I'll tell you another thing," said Joss.

"Isn't that enough for me to be going on with for now?"

"No, it isn't. You know your sister?"

"Where does she come into it?"

"She can go to the sanatorium. What have you got to say to that Miss Jones?"

My mother had very little to say. It was all too much for her to take in.

"My mouth is dry with surprise," she said at last. And she went on the steps of the pump, and cupped her hands under the spout. Joss was still leaning against the dome.

"Well come on," she said. "Standing there. It's your turn to work the handle."

Everybody's story can have a happy ending if it is stopped at a chosen point. I end my mother's when she was happiest of all accepting my father's roundabout proposal that evening by the pump.

SKIN DEEP

I hadn't realised that I'd become such an oddity in my own parish, until the lady refugee from the riots, who has come to the old cottage, pointed out that I'd survived from the age of the water-wheel and the flail to that of the space probe, and she suggested that I should write an autobiography and make money. That's all very well, but I'd be hard put to remember what my mother said when she came to the Big Barn and saw us swinging the billy-goat by his horns on a hay rope attached to the crossbeams, though I do recall she was annoyed.

Nor can I remember what I said when I went with my father to attend to young Anne Roberts, after she'd shot herself in the corner of the hayfield one June morning, when the sun was starting a long, warm day and her blood and the dew were mixed on the grass.

Of my life I see only certain days and happenings, and people to whom the things were happening, and those days are not necessarily times of joy or triumph or great sadness. They are like one spoke of the spinning-wheel that you see for one moment due to the refraction of the light. They just stand out of the great mist — that's all.

But while I'd been pondering thus, the lady had been talking about immigration, a subject upon which she had strong views since she'd changed parishes, and I could not then but remember Black Man One Tooth; the first of all who came.

He was the Indian pedlar of silks who walked the countryside from door-to-door. He came from Bangor I believe, and wound round his head he had a pink turban, which my mother called a pudding cloth. On top of that he carried his merchandise in a large leather case, until he looked from afar like a capital T. He had one yellow tooth in the corner of his mouth like a wild boar, and Now Bach's father, who had been a soldier, said there were some large birds in India that came out after dark to extract the teeth of people who slept with their mouths open; but he had few believers in the village, ever since that time he saw John the Baptist waiting for the bus by the corner of the hearse house, one wild night when he was coming home from Pen-y-Bont hotel.

But no one knew very much about the black man, apart from the fact that he wore a long overcoat summer and winter, and if he was seen without that, it was as good a sign as seeing the Conwy mist that we were in for some settled weather.

Old Siani, who lived alongside the Smithy, maintained he was of a good family from Bombay, only he'd done something against their religion, like putting his boot under the backside of a cow or some trivial thing like that.

Even so, it didn't dispel the awe in which he was held by the village children and some of their mothers, and indeed, there were some fearful tales circulating about him at school, especially what he had in his bag, while Tomos Owen, Tŷ Newydd, had gone as far as to suggest that he was a great one for the women.

Some said he had a cutlass in his bag, and that he had threatened Margiad Hughes with it, when she refused to buy a petticoat that was half as cheap again as any she could find on the Square in Caernarfon on Saturdays. And Bob the milkman said he'd been seen in Bryn Madog field shooting at acorns with a revolver.

And what I knew myself was this. My mother was in the living kitchen one morning at the old farm, blackleading the grate, when there came a knock at the door. "Come in," she said, thinking it was Old Siani come for her eggs, but to her surprise, when she got to her feet, who should be standing there in the middle of the floor but Black Man One Tooth.

He slapped his bag on the table and undid the straps, and she could do no less than buy a blouse off him to send him on his way, and while she was fetching the money from the sideboard drawer in the front room, she didn't for a moment let go of her blacklead brush. He became a plague after that — that's to say — until he had that scuff-uff with Aunty Nell, and it was shortly after that it was discovered he had something seven times worse in his bag than weapons of war.

Aunty Nell was a peg-leg blood relation of my mother's, a small body with boot button eyes, and she had once been imprisoned on Ellis Island when she tried to go to America on a bad passport. She had also spoken to the Prime Minister of the Little People at the stile of the Meadow of the Water Reeds, and he'd promised her a fortune later on in life for putting milk out for the Little People every night.

Well, anyway, she was turning out under the stairs when Black Man One Tooth arrived and set his case down on the threshold.

"We don't want anything thank you," said Aunty Nell.

"You're not the missus," he said.

"I'm the missus today," she replied, and threw an old wellington at him, and if he hadn't been quick at ducking, he'd have caught the sole on his forehead.

Of course, I took the story to school, and it was known to everyone by the last bell that Aunty Nell was the boss of Black Man One Tooth; but within a couple of days Now Bach had brought another to trump all that had gone before, and make everyone ten times more afraid than ever.

His mother had come home one day, sick as a dog — and it wasn't the time for her migraine either. She was coming home from the Round Shop across the Meadow of the Water Reeds, and when she came to the last kissing gate, there was Black Man One Tooth, sitting with his back to the Barn of the White Stones. His bag was open on the path in front of him, and standing straight up out of that was a large snake.

That in itself had been enough to make Now's mother drop her baskets and run all the way round Arthur Terrace. But she had seen something that was more horrifying. The black man was stark naked.

When she plucked up courage to tell the whole story to her husband when he came home from work, he was quite offhand about it. Didn't she realise it was terribly dangerous to charm snakes when you were fully clothed? The snake wouldn't recognise its master and would bite him in an instant. He would slough his skin then every round year for the rest of his life — if indeed he lived at all.

When I asked Now what colour the snake was, he said he hadn't thought of asking, but he was almost sure it was a yellow one with green eyes. I looked in that nature book that my mother had bought at Doctor Roberts' auction, but I couldn't find a single creature anywhere approaching the description, and when I told Now, he said that the black man had probably sent away for it, like his mother did when she fancied anything in the catalogue.

We didn't see Black Man One Tooth again for a baking or two; until midsummer in fact. The bog cotton was swaying in the still heat, and in the evenings the swifts were screaming high in the great air oceans, when who should come over the mountain from Bethesda for his holidays at the old farm, with his nightshirt under his arm, but Dei Braichmelyn, whose father was second cousin to my mother.

He was older than me and venturesome. He had once gone astride the ridges of the farm buildings, all round the yard and over the Big Barn without once setting foot on the ground. And my mother said that he had brought shame on the family when he put his grandmother's cockerel through the mangle one washday.

He'd been running errands and saving up, and we went to the Round Shop to buy a Woodbine five, pretending it was for Jack Pensarn who happened to be singling turnips for my father. We were on the way back when Black Man One Tooth came out behind us from Tŷ Gwyn yard.

I felt like making a bolt for it straightaway, but of course I couldn't leave Dei to the mercies of the snake. So I stuck it out even though he was gaining on us, and I could feel the prickles running down my back, until we heard him turning down the path to the house of Robin Bilws.

We went on and jumped over into the Meadow of the Water Reeds, to light up and blow smoke through our nostrils, and I thought it as good a time as any to tell Dei about the cutlass and the snake. But he wasn't the least bit impressed. The black man came to Bethesda too sometimes, he said, and he was known in that area as Jack Black, and he was as harmless as a new born lamb.

Presently, we heard him padding by muttering to himself, and we crouched behind the wall. I was anxious then to get in front of him to warn my mother so that she could slam the door and bolt it, but he turned down the other path, and, on the slate footbridge that crossed the ditch, he sat himself down and opened his case. Then he began to take his clothes off.

We were both staring at the case expecting to see the snake appear, and I could hear Dei sucking his breath. Instead of that, Black Man One Tooth jumped into the ditch with his pudding cloth still on his head.

"He's going for a dip," said Dei.

But the black man realised his mistake too late. There is no solid bed to the peat ditches like there is to Mother Ganges. He was down to his armpits in a minute and shouting like a jackass.

"The old goat is going to drown," said Dei, and we both ran to the edge of the ditch, all fear forgotten in the emergency, and just in time we were. There was barely his turban in sight, and he was on his way to those places under the earth.

We grabbed his arms, and he held on like a vice, and it became evident that if we were not going to pull him out, he was determined to take us with him the other way. We had a hard struggle of it, and I distinctly remember seeing — as one does take notice of irrelevant things at such times — a blue dragonfly coasting past.

At last we got him out, and he brought a barrow load of peat with him which made him a shade blacker than he was ever meant to be. He lay there on his side like a wet calf, and we were sitting about him in the grass, panting like old engines. It was then that I noticed that he had been wrongly christened. He had at least two other teeth at the back of his mouth.

Then suddenly he stood up, lean as a heron, spread his arms out, and began to preach at us in some strange language. Dei said after that he was thanking us in his own way, but we didn't stay for the translation. Off we scampered like goats in a thunderstorm, and we didn't stop until we were well behind the rick in the Big Barn. When we at last ventured to peep round the corner, we saw him getting his things together and placing his bag on his head and his trousers on his arm.

Just then we heard my mother calling the men to supper with the big conch. And we too went in. Jack and Robin Sam and Cariad Yw were sitting round the table with us in the milk-house.

When Mother brought in the butter-milk jugs and the potatoes, she said,

"I saw the old black man this afternoon. He was going along the path. I could have sworn he had no trousers on."

Dei and me just kept our noses low in our bowls and said nothing.

THE GUEST

We lived at the old farm then, below the Bluestone Quarry, which is now a power-station so that our ways can be lit cheaper than by rushlight.

The gypsies came then too, I remember, to the Lane of the Sky. There was a steep pitch at the top end before it was flattened, and hazel trees grew like a tunnel, so that when you looked uphill, the lane seemed to end in the sky, like that ladder that Jacob dreamt about in the long ago time.

The gypsies came twice a year: in the Spring and Menai Bridge Fair time. They had half a dozen horse-drawn *vardos,* beautifully painted and chamfered, and they carried everything with them, like hens and goats and rabbits — and they brought Rosa Boswell.

She was the object of my adoration for a while, although it was said at school that Gwen, Chapel House, was my sweetheart; but how was I to know that she would get as fat as her mother?

I had orders however not to go near the gypsies, and that rhyme used to go through my head like a rondo:

'My mother said, I never should,
Play with the gypsies in the wood.'

But I had to go past their pitch to get conkers from the copse, and as it so often happens in life, the candle flame is stronger than the moth.

The people of the parish round about were just a little bit afraid of them, but they need not have been. They were ten times safer with *them* than with some they've got about them today. The women went round selling pegs and telling fortunes, and when Margiad Anne's mother slammed the garden gate on them, her clothes-basket took fire.

My father set one or two of the gypsy men to work casually with seasonal duties, and he gave them old iron and folds of hay from the rick, but it was just as well to clap a blind eye to a turnip disappearing from the field, or a horse being turned into the pasture overnight. And they left no filth behind them like their imitators, just a black fire circle.

But the strangest thing was, you would never see them arrive nor depart. Either they were in the Lane or they were not.

I was reading *Lavengro* then, and it was small effort to connect this crew with the inhabitants of that book: Tawno Chikno, and Grey Moll, and Ursula; and sometimes I could see old Borrow himself coming down the Lane with his book under his arm to get his boxing lessons from Jasper Petulengro.

But it was in the Smithy that I first saw Rosa Boswell. It was a wet day in October. My parents had gone to market in the Morris Bull Nose, and I had been given orders to take the grey nosed pony to be shod; and there I was, hanging on the handle of the big bellows blowing a nice shaping fire, and Richiard Hughes was talkative and in a good temper because he had caught eighteen rats that very morning in his barrel, and I counted them too, lying side by side round the back like soldiers after Loos, and ready to be put on the fire at going home time to bank it up overnight.

There was a plague of rats in the Smithy then. I suppose there is more tasty bait to attract them today, but then they were partial to hoof parings; and so bad had they become that Siani, who lived next-door to the workshop, went to bed in her clothes, with an ash-plant alongside her to swipe them in the night. And some had the fear that if something were to happen to her at dead of night there would be nothing left of her by morning, only back-bone, like a herring.

But Richiard Hughes was better at dealing with them. He had made a patent catch-them-alive with an old treacle barrel and a little see-saw which he had built into its side. He had a bit of bait at the end of the see-saw, and it tilted and came back again. It was nothing to see a dozen to fifteen rats in a scrum on the bottom in the morning. Then he would boil water in that big iron kettle and pour it over them.

Old Siani herself used to come in some days for a warm, or for a couple of red coals when she felt like having a fire herself, and when she didn't, which was more often than not, she would bring some jacket potatoes and set them near the fire on the forge, or a pot of broth, and even a sheep's head when things had gone well.

When things were fairly slack, Richiard Hughes would roll up his leather apron and rest a thigh on the anvil, listening to Siani's reports of the outlying farms, where she went for eggs and butter and a *stelc* in the ingle-nook to quiz the maids and praise the mistress. And sometimes she would tell of the Smithy ghost that blew the big bellows in the night, and there was sure to be something in it, for if you let the handle down last thing, it would often be up in the morning.

Richiard Hughes was telling me this and more besides, when a girl came out of the rain through the half-door, with her hair streaming water, and as black as the forge side, I knew then that the gypsies had come. She went up to the fire and her clothes began to steam.

"I want some old horseshoes," she said, just like that, and she wasn't much older than I was.

Richiard Hughes took little notice. He kept on banging the anvil, and she said not another word. It was evident though that she meant to stay until going home time in order to get what she wanted, and when the sparks were flying in all directions, she didn't shut her eyes nor turn her head one little bit.

I was ready to go then, and Richiard Hughes began to ferret in the corners and he found her some old shoes. Then she came after me up the hill, saying uncomplimentary things about the pony, that she had a better and faster one by far, and she didn't need a saddle to ride it either. But I knew what her sore was: she wanted to ride it herself. I've always been soft with women so I told her to jump up behind, which she did in a minute still clutching her horseshoes. She smelt of wood smoke, but it was like perfume then.

All the same, I'd expected her to jump off at the entrance to the Lane of the Sky, but she had no intention of doing so. She stuck on until we were in our yard by the stable door. It was then that I began to doubt the wisdom of bringing her, because, as soon as we were inside, she was into everything like a terrier, and

67

she fancied that plaited whip with the bone handle that my uncle had when he was a *gaucho* in Patagonia.

She wanted to go through the whole steading then, and the servants' loft, and I got anxious when she ran into the chicken house, because I knew that her family were partial to fried eggs, and she wouldn't be beyond thrusting a few eggs into her apron pockets. She went poking in the boiler shed too where the feeding stuffs were kept in bags all round the walls, and she must have thought it was the cornucopia, for I saw her eyes widen, and she put her hand into the Indian corn bag and slammed it into her mouth.

It was still pelting outside and water was coming out of the downspouts like Niagara Falls, and I didn't feel like puddling about in the cold, I wanted my tea, so while she was busybodying in the shed I managed to get the house key from under the slate, and then I had to ask her in because she was my guest. But when she came into the living kitchen, you would have thought that she had stumbled on Captain Morgan's treasure; she began to finger the candlesticks and the pewterware on the old dresser and to ask all kinds of questions about them like the Inquisition.

Next thing, she was in the front room, standing in front of the brass-faced grandfather clock and her head was moving to the rhythm of the pendulum, and I suppose for two pins she would have slung it on her shoulder and taken it to her people in the Lane of the Sky.

It was then that I thought I had better do something about it. If my parents happened to arrive home from market and see her there, fingering their property, they would both be seeing Ireland. So, I filled a glass with butter-milk, and held it in front of her and backed away, as if I was enticing a weaned calf to a trough, and she came round the corner to the milk-house, but I had made a bad mistake. Hanging there above her head was the salted meat, and her mind immediately turned towards food. It was then that she told me she was partial to hedgehogs too, but as we didn't have any of those, in or out of salt, she had to make do with a slice of bread and a *talbo* of cheese, and she took them through to the living kitchen by the fire as if she was paying rent for the whole place.

But say what you like, it was a romantic age.

"Why are your eyes so blue and your hair so yellow?" she asked me all of a sudden.

"I don't know," I said. "Why are yours so black?"

She got hold of the steel poker and pushed it into the fire. Then she told me that she had just been to her aunt's funeral near Shrewsbury, and after they had buried her, they came back and burned her things, her *vardo* and everything.

"That's a pity," I remember saying. "What a waste too."

Up she sprang like a shot hare.

"None of your business," she said. "I'm going now, and I shan't be coming back to drink your old butter-milk either. It's too sour."

And by then I didn't know whether I wanted her to go or not, but go she did, and as things would have it, straight to face my parents coming home in the Morris Bull Nose round the Churning Pond bend.

When my mother came in, wet, and a bit tired, she wanted to know why I hadn't spread the tea. "What did that girl want?" she asked.

"Begging." I said.

"You don't want to 'tice that crew, or we won't have anything left on post nor pillar."

Half an hour later when we were having our tea, there came a knock at the door. It was Rosa Boswell come to look for her horseshoes, and when my mother found them, they were on the churn-bench in the milk-house. And I had a terrible job explaining how they came to be there in the first place.

Swaying as I am now on my aged heels, I can't help wondering now and again: Have they burned the *vardo* of Rosa Boswell?

TROTTERS

My father kept two sows that farrowed alternately, which meant that we had a new litter of piglets every six months or so, and they were sold at six weeks as weaners to the smallholders at twenty five shillings a head for fattening. They were always in demand like Cwm-y-Glo cakes, and that was just as well, at a time when everyone had to rely on his own efforts to make ends meet and not on the government.

But it's easier written than wrought. Pig rearing at best I found has its complications. The first stages could be dodgy, even perilous.

There were definite signs when the piglets were on their way. The sow would start to carry straw and twigs like a magpie into corners where they were least required to be, and she had to be forcibly persuaded sometimes that the sty after all was the best place for her confinement.

My father rigged a bar, a foot from the wall, to prevent the sow lying too close and crushing her offspring. Gilts that were new to the experience would jump up at the least squeal; but older sows grew indifferent, and on occasions, if not watched, would eat their young.

Straw would be piled on the floor and a milking stool fetched for the watcher. The storm-lantern would be primed and hung out of harm's way for late night emergencies. Those were the laid down basics for successful pig midwifery.

I've sat into the night-watches many times with sows in the sty, while the lantern threw silhouettes of witches and cherubs on the wall. My father on such a watch when a boy, dozed off in the straw in the dead hours of early morning. When he woke, the sow had already farrowed and the litter was well and sucking, but he never let on when my grandfather arrived a few minutes later. It wouldn't do. It was a matter of honour to keep awake.

But there was another part to it which was no less daunting. The sows had to be taken to the boar, and he was kept at a farm near the Menai Straits, and I was usually the one who took them. But I've seen one or two go on their own, and even jumping clean out of the sty as the spirit took them. They would trot along under the hedgerows, snatching at tufts of grass that took their fancy, and one even went over into the grounds of the Big Inn and started to plough the lawn.

It was the old sow that decided to travel overnight that caused the commotion. She met the people coming away from evening chapel, and the two old Miss. Joneses fled up the path and took refuge in Cae Dicwm cart-house, and they wouldn't come out until somebody was able to persuade them that it wasn't a crocodile broken out from Hendre marsh.

When I drove the sows, my father used to tie a length of rope to their fetlocks, and I wound the other end round my hand, and opening the sty door was like springing the traps at a greyhound meeting. There was no stopping after that. You had to go, and keep going like a tin tied to a dog's tail. I had no hope of stopping them once they were started, because they weighed twice as much as I did then. The only purpose of the rope was to serve as a brake to retard them while I had a chance to run in front and turn their heads in the other direction. Even so, it was touch and go. Once they got their snouts between your legs you found yourself astride their backs in no time, and riding in the swine Derby the wrong way round.

My two worries on the drive were the churchyard, and the quarry railway-crossing further down, where the sow could bolt into the path of an oncoming train, and be made into bacon slices without going to Denmark.

Once I took a gilt down on a very hot day, I remember, and she was poking her snout everywhere but where it should have been, and she dragged me into Tan Dinas hollow, and there she flopped on her side in the cold stream. There was no shifting her for a spell, but when she finally went, she went, and in two minutes flat we were by the parish pump.

I had a mind to have some cooling water myself by then, and I tried to whip the rope round the stem of the pump, to hold the gilt while I put my mouth to the spout; but when I began to pump the handle, she started to squeal, and she pulled the rope clean out of my hand, and off she went uphill in the direction of the church. When I got to the top after her there was a row of funeral carriages outside the churchyard gate, and I was just in time to see the sow trotting up to the church door, but at the last minute she had second thoughts, turned under the yew tree and disappeared.

When I reached the corner, I found that it would have been ten times better if she had gone her original way. The mourners were by then congregated at the graveside; Mr Morgan Jones the parson was reading over it, and I saw the sow going towards them, as if she had been invited to attend as one of the family, and I didn't know what on earth to do.

She was rooting round their heels, and by then some of them were taking more notice of her antics than the burial service itself. A man at last snatched the rope, but in two minutes he was sorry he'd meddled. The sow made a deft swerve round the corner of a *cist* and dragged him face down on the inscription. He was glad to let go, and the sow fled to the far boundary wall. When I plucked enough nerve to go after her, she was chewing some flowers that someone had left in a glass jar.

By the time I had chased her two or three times up and down the boundary wall, the mourners luckily, had gone, because when I finally got hold of the rope, we started another sprint, right across, back towards the church, in and out of kerbs and headstones. Fortunately there were two men with black bowlers on the path, and they took those off for the second time that day, and waved them about, which turned the sow towards the gate, or God knows, I might have been penned in there with her for a week.

Just then, who came out of the church porch but John Williams the sexton. He was in his best black, and he started a lecture about little boys who should on no account be let loose to drive pigs on the King's Highway. But the sow didn't want to stay and listen to him developing his thesis. Off we bounded like staghounds along the road, and all I could do was to keep on running and quietly give thanks that we were at least pointing in the right direction.

Down towards the sea we travelled at a constant trot, nearer and nearer to that other bogey: the quarry railway-crossing. There was an old pensioner in charge of it then, who had nothing else to do in between trains but count the flies on the window-panes of his hut and waylay innocents like me. He used to lean on the half-door, shouting questions after me, and I was hard put to answer over my shoulder, as I was being plucked further and further out of earshot.

"Going to the boar are you? How's your mother?" Never any mention of my father. "Have you started on the haymaking?" or seeding clover, or whatever the seasonal activity was.

But it was difficult to socialise, and had the sow taken it into her head to swim the Straits, I would probably have been the first water-skier to cross to Anglesey.

Griffith Jones was the name of the boar keeper. He had been to sea, and was a good hand at untying knots, which was lucky for me, because by then, the knot on the sow's leg had gone so tight that I could have sworn it had been welded, and my hand had been so long bound by the rope that it had become stiff until it looked half-withered like the hand of that man in the Bible.

I had to leave the sow at the farm for a few days sometimes, and on the way back I tried to sneak past the crossing, but I never managed to dodge the old man who had the vigilance of the lonely soul.

"Come in, come in," he would say. "The night will come just the same." And he would put the kettle on his bit of fire. "You'll have a cup of tea to take you along."

But he was not very well equipped to handle guests. He had a large tin mug, which had I suppose started off as blue as the sky, inside and out — before the detergent men had started their apprenticeship. I was usually parched after my run, but one look at that convinced me that I wasn't so thirsty after all.

And he had some stories to tell about pigs, enough to raise the hair on my head, and make me think twice before going within a hundred yards of any pig again.

There was a little maid servant on an Anglesey farm, he told me, whose work it was to feed the pigs, and amongst them there was a spiteful old sow. When the girl was bent over the trough pouring out the feed, the sow took a bite at her arm like a shark, and cut it right off. "And all the poor girl could do," he said, "was stand there with the bucket in her other hand, watching the sow eating her arm."

I never mentioned at home that I had stopped at the hut with the old man, or I would have been for it, because I was expected back straightaway to report that the sow had arrived at the other end safely.

How would I get on nowadays if I drove a pig down the road on a rope? I suppose they would have a police car in front with flashing lights to make sure we wouldn't both end up permanently in Llanddeiniolen churchyard.

ON A SHINING NIGHT

It's not such a long time ago that my uncle had to leave the country when he was caught poaching pheasants. My grandfather was given the choice of sending him away, or losing the old farm. Rather than see them all turned out, my uncle went to Patagonia where he became a *gaucho* for a time. After that, he went to Australia where he had a sheep-farm. In the First War he came back with the New South Wales Light Infantry to fight for the system that had sent him away. He was killed at Hangard Woods on the Somme, thereby safeguarding for me the privilege of carrying on the same old custom in this parish.

I suppose it is safe to confess now that I used to go to the spinneys with my gun on moonlight nights to wait for the pheasants to come in from the stubble. You could hear them fluttering up the trees to roost, and their silhouettes could be seen in the bare branches against the gloaming. But getting close enough to them was another matter. You had to go into the wood with the wind facing, and I've shot a few birds and lost them again when they fell into the dark undergrowth.

One night I was in Rhydau covert, and I shot two cocks in a matter of minutes. It was a bright, quiet night, silver and blue, and the reports and flashes from the gun made you think that the heavens were about to fall.

When I was arranging my burden I heard a stick break under a heavy foot, and I knew that there was someone standing between me and safety, so to throw them off the scent, I ran in another direction and made for Old Siani's cot by the Smithy.

She was swaying on her old heels then Siani, and I knew that she would be abed as soon as the dusk came on winter nights, to save candles and heating. Once, when some roisterers had plastered her windows with cow-dung in the night, she was in bed for a whole day waiting for it to get light.

"Who's there?" I heard her call from the bedchamber when I banged on the door. Presently, I heard her removing the bolts like the jailer of the Bastille, and I saw her head peering round the door in the moonlight.

"Is there someone after you?" she asked as I blundered my way inside over the old chairs she had in the little lobby.

"Go back to bed," I said. "I shan't be staying long."

But she was determined not to go without knowing what I had with me, and she insisted upon feeling the birds' breasts.

I flung myself down on that old wooden settle with the cocks on my knee, and she returned to the bedchamber. Even though it was pretty dark inside, I knew very well what kind of a place it was, because I went there often to take the farm butter. I knew there would be a pile of faggots between the back of the settle and the dresser, and in the far corner there was a grandfather clock stopped at twenty past ten, but that didn't worry Siani one bit. She had buried two husbands and reached threescore and five by frugality alone, and she wasn't bothered whether it was midnight or noon that the clock was striking, even when it was going.

She had found another use for it. There were half a dozen umbrellas hanging on its face, and above the sailing-ship that had swung on its blue sea at every round second, there was a pile of shepherd's purse.

There was a slate slab across the chimney-breast to hide a large dent, so Richiard Hughes maintained, where the big bellows used to be when the cottage was a workshop in the long ago time. And on the hearth there was a small round table, and one cup and a jamjar in which Siani made tea with the same tea-leaves from one week's end to the next, because using a teapot had no part in her economics.

Above my head I knew there were bundles of herbs hanging

76

from the beams, a policeman's lantern, and a musket. The rest of the place appeared in daylight as if a bolt of lightning had entered and couldn't find its way out again.

There was a belief in the parish that she was hoarding money, and people said that Now Bach's mother had gone there one afternoon for a *clatch*, and she'd seen something rolling out of the bottom of the clock, and, even though she had to wear glasses as thick as the bottom of a jamjar, she swore that it was a yellow sovereign.

But if she was frugal and a bit apart, she wasn't lonely Old Siani. In the summer you would see her in the lanes talking to the flowers and the birds, and at night her house was swarming with rats.

While I was sitting like that on the settle, I heard footsteps outside in the road, stopping and going on again.

"Was that one after you?" asked Siani from her bed, but I said not a word only listened, and just then I heard rats scampering all about me, and one ran over my foot: I suspected that they had smelt the birds. I wasn't feeling comfortable by a long way.

"Haven't you got a candle somewhere?" I asked, but she didn't want to waste tallow until I told her I had a match.

By the light of a bit of moon that stole in through the little window, I found a piece of candle on the mantelpiece, and after I had lit that, the rats withdrew for a bit; but just then, when I happened to look in the direction of the big clock, I saw the head and shoulders of a monster rat sticking out of the hole that was in the skirting and I could feel the skin on my neck tightening, because it had a mane like a mountain-pony.

I reached for the gun, put a cartridge in, and when its head appeared again, I let go a shot right across the room until the whole place was shaking and reeking with the smell of cordite. I heard Siani scream like a hare in a hang, and the next thing she was at the chamber door with her cudgel in her hand looking like Buddug when she was chasing the Romans.

"What are you doing to my house?" she shouted. "Get off home with you before I put this across your neck! It would have been ten times better if I'd let those keepers in. At least they would have respected my things. I'd never open for you again, even if you had a gang of demons at your heels."

But open she did, and that the very next morning, because when she calmed down, I persuaded her to let me leave my gun and the cocks on top of the dresser overnight, in case I bumped into someone I shouldn't on my way home.

There was hoar-frost that morning, and I remember going with a bag under my arm filled with potatoes for the old and the needy, and I was expecting a scolding. But Siani was in high spirits, and the first thing she said was:

"D'you know what? You'll have to come oftener with that gun. Those old rats left me pretty well alone all night." And I had difficulty in persuading her not to make tea in her jampot.

"Listen," I said. "You'd better keep one of those cocks."

She became more elated still and even lit a small fire.

"I'll start on it right away," she said, and off she went round the back to fetch her wash-tub. Then she sat across the hearth and began plucking the bird into the tub, but she had made sure that the door was bolted.

"Do you know what I'm afraid of," she said, "that you'll be caught and transported like your uncle!"

"No fear," I said. "They've stopped doing things like that now."

"But they still hang people don't forget."

And just then there was a report like a gunshot right above our heads. The slate across the chimney-breast split in two like the temple curtain, and it dropped like two guillotines on the fender and the iron stools, and before we realised what was happening, a boulder came tumbling out of the chimney like a new laid egg. It bounced on the edge of the grate and the wash-tub and upset the round table, and the cup and the jamjar, and smashed them to bits on the floor.

I don't know exactly what I did while all that was happening, but when I recovered sufficiently to take notice, there was Siani, on the floor all mixed-up with the tub and the feathers, leaning her back on the bottom of the settle and chewing the corner of her apron. Neither of us spoke for a few minutes. But in the end she said:

"You and these old rats have bewitched the place."

At the time I could only believe that she meant it. In the end when she got to her feet, we managed to roll the boulder out through the door, and Siani said that a dish of tea would restore us, and when I think of it, there was at least one blessing that came out of it all — she found a brand new jamjar, clean and shining to make tea.

The hole in the breasting however, stayed there for months, but that didn't worry Siani, because she was not overfond of fires, and no wonder. Her fuel supply depended on the passage of horses up and down the road. When she died, she was worth thousands, and I for one was not surprised.

But I remember what my father said when I went home with only one cock-pheasant, and I told him how I had given Siani the other as a reward for shelter the previous night.

"You're too weak with women," he said. "You won't be able to buy yourself out of every pickle with a pheasant you know."

"Do you think so?" I said, country-soft.

But by now, I know another thing. He was right.

INTO THE MIST

When we lived at the old farm under Snowdon in the thirties, our lives were fairly secure within the fabric of our own community, where codes were rigid, and based on goodwill and the division of capital. Neighbouring farms sent men and implements to help with the seasonal activities, and even maids were lent and borrowed, and interest in kind paid for their services. Favours were recorded and returned; either in one piece or by instalments. It was pretty near a *soviet* in its own unwitting way, operating within what was left of the Feudal System.

Our boundary neighbour was Robert Owen, Fron. He was a middle-aged bachelor who lived with his mother. He was a good friend and loyal. He sent two men to the threshing and the shearing where others sent one, and he was a frequent visitor himself. He came to see my father one day and asked:

"Can this boy do an errand for me?"

He explained that he'd had a mind for some time to get a little maid to help his mother, and at the Pwllheli hiring fair, he'd had wind of one; an orphan girl who was at a place the other side of Snowdon at the time, but she wanted to leave at the end of the season.

"She's coming over the mountain tomorrow," he said. "And she won't be sure of her way on this side. Will the boy go to meet her?"

It was mid-morning when I started for the mountain. It was a hazy day towards the end of September, and I had orders not to go any further than the limit of our sheepwalk. I took with me some bread and cheese and a raw egg; standard sustenance for those working far from the steading. I was so afraid of smashing the egg, that I struck it against my teeth and swallowed it before I got to the quarry pits. Then I followed the river as far as the waterfall where I'd ventured once hoping to meet Lorna Doone. I sat there by the pool, and the foam from the falls was swirling on its surface before being broken into pieces like elderblossom and snatched away by the stream. I dozed watching that, and when I woke, the sun had taken the day a considerable way towards Ireland. I heard a curlew calling, and I moved higher and sat in a cranny, and I ate some of my bread and cheese. I could see the farms dotted below, all around the old Celtic Fort; the far side of Anglesey I could see, and Man, and even the blue rim of the Wicklow Hills of Ireland. I strained my eyes to sweep the far slope, but I could see no movement there. Now the evening was coming up at me from the floor of the land, and I felt like giving up and starting back, but I was charged with a duty to bring the maid.

Then I saw the Conwy mist. It was coming slowly along the ground from the Bethesda side, over the ridge in a cylindrical bar like a python, and I knew that if I stayed I would be directly in its path, and I would be swallowed in it. I went higher again to avoid it, and when I looked round, I saw the maid coming down the far slope a mile away. I waved and called, even knowing that she would not hear, and she was directly in the way of the mist before she realised, and was swallowed into it out of sight.

I ran along the edge of the mist calling all the time, but there was no answer. I was enough of an old mountain-hand however to stay where I was, for I knew that the width of the bar of mist might extend as far as the quarry pits, and I feared for the maid. I stopped calling then and watched the mist sliding silently by, and in the last of the daylight, the top of the mountain behind me looked like a gladiator's helmet. Then, directly below where I stood, the girl walked out of the mist, and she appeared surprised at seeing me.

"I was sent to meet you," I said. "I called, you didn't hear."

"No matter," she said, setting her box down and sitting on it. "What's your name?"

"John."

"Oh." She wore an old straw bonnet and she had black hair. "We'll be all right then, you'll see."

"How is that?"

"My name is Mary. We are both in the Bible."

She was fifteen she said. She spoke in the long vowelled dialect of Llŷn. It was new to me but I found it endearing. I gave her the remainder of my bread, and she was glad of it.

"We shall have to stay for a while," I said. "The Conwy mist takes about an hour to pass. It's a sign of fair weather."

We spent the time in question and answer. She seemed to be more interested in the old farm than she was in her destination, and I was not short in telling her everything about it. When the mist finally drew its tail, we walked down and I was carrying her box.

"If we didn't have a little maid already, you could have come to us," I said.

When we arrived at the old farm the moon was up, and we were just in time to forestall the men setting out to look for us, and it was decided that Mary Jones should go no further that night. She was put in the boxroom to sleep with Jenny Price, our little maid, and in the morning they were both up betimes, vying with each other to light the fires and fetch water with the yokes.

After she'd had breakfast, I accompanied Mary Jones across the marshes to her new home, still carrying her box, but I was reluctant to leave her. I never admitted as much, but the chances were that I was in love with Mary Jones. That is why I so looked forward to her visits to the old farm, for come she did, quite often, and the way she and Jenny Price sized each other up, was comical to behold.

Gradually and without prompting, Mary Jones revealed her story to my mother, who she had evidently appointed her confidante. She was alone in the world. Her parents had died from tuberculosis, and she had no worldly goods other than her box and her Bible, and a little blue porcelain vinaigrette. She brought it to show one day, carefully wrapped in cotton wool.

She seemed to be happy with Robert Owen and his mother, and they were well satisfied with her. It was never mentioned that she was expected to give additional services after hours, as was considered commonplace, especially in bachelor households. But she said one day that she had a great fear of the well. It appeared that when she was letting down the bucket on the windlass, she could see her reflection far down in the water. The image did not seem to be quite her own, and it seemed to beckon. My mother calmed her by saying that she was at a certain age, and that it was a passing thing. And so it proved.

Mary Jones soon had other things to occupy her mind however, and the change came about after threshing day at the old farm. Mother, given no doubt to the superstition of the times, attributed ensuing events directly to the happenings of that day.

The threshing gang had congregated early in the October morning. The frost was already curling the brown leaves into little balls underfoot, and the marsh mists were hanging over the peat-hags. Amongst the crew was Will Davies, Rhydau Farm, strong and of good farming skills. His father was ailing then, and he had charge of the farm. It was said that he was looking for a wife.

There were three or four women in the house with my mother. Mary Jones was there too helping to prepare the threshing dinner, and when Will came into the front room for his, it was noticed by those whose duty it is to perceive, that they didn't take the blindest bit of notice of each other. It came as no surprise then to learn later that they were keeping company.

There was also present a man who had slept the previous night in the barn. There were many people on the roads then, and for their accommodation it was an unwritten rule that they did a turn of work in the morning.

This man however was not of the common run of tramps. He purported to be a bookseller, indeed he carried a bundle of books with him, tied with a strap. He was peculiarly dressed too in a floppy hat and a cape, and he was effeminate, which tended to make him a figure of fun in such a masculine community. He was quite prepared to do his turn of work with the threshing box, but it was obvious that he was not used to heavy labour. My father set him on with me, raking the husks as they were shaken out of the belly of the box. Later, after reading Matthew Arnold, I've always seen him as the Scholar Gypsy.

But he spoke the Llŷn dialect, and at table he exchanged remarks with Mary Jones about some village they both seemed familiar with down the Peninsula. In spite of this, or because of it, Will Davies tended to decry him more than the rest.

Early one morning, some weeks later, Robert Owen came

to the old farm to say that Mary Jones had not come home the previous night. The men went out to look for her the whole day on the marshes and in the copses. I don't know in what condition they expected to find her, but she was not found, nor has she ever been.

There were many theories advanced about her disappearance, from the possibility that she was with child, to the extreme suggestion of self-destruction. I knew that my mother secretly, to the very end was convinced that she was at the bottom of the well. Neither was the bookseller seen again, although people from the parish occasionally went down Llŷn and to the Pwllheli hiring fair.

But Mother, in the spring time, was cleaning out the milk-house. In the corner of the wide slate window-sill, she reached out to remove what she thought was a lump of mildew, but it was cotton-wool. Inside it was Mary Jones's blue porcelain vinaigrette. I have it still.

GLEANERS' HARVEST

Old Siani who lived by the Smithy in the long ago time, had an orphan child to live with her once. Her name was Lisabeth Davies, but everyone called her Lisi Bach. She had flame-coloured hair and emerald eyes, and although she was no more than eight years old then, it was evident that she would grow into a beautiful woman.

Adoption I suppose they would call that arrangement today, but then, it was more like buying a dog. There were no forms to fill, nor officials to arrive to inspect the accommodation to see if it was suitable for a child's comfort and health. If that had been the case, I'm sure no one would have allowed the girl within a mile of the place to live amongst all that disorder and the rats.

But Siani saw nothing out of place in it. She treated Lisi as if she had been born there, and looked upon her as some kind of little maid, to fetch and carry, and run errands in between going to school at Llanbabo, and she wouldn't have been sent there either, if it wasn't for the school attendance officer who went looking for her every other week.

She would be about my age Lisi Bach, and I remember exactly to the day the time she came; it was Palm Sunday, and Siani brought her to the old farm next day, to show her, like a kitten. But she soon had a taste for coming on her own to fetch eggs and butter, and to play with me, and she hated going home; she scraped all kinds of excuses for staying, and so fond was she of her freedom, that she came across the fields without leave, and my mother often used to send her home, knowing full well that Siani knew nothing of her whereabouts. But I didn't get to know until later, that Mother had another reason for keeping her at arm's length. Her head was boiling with lice.

All the same, she was not an easy one to fob off, and in the end, for the sake of her own comfort and other people's ease of mind, my mother decided to tackle the lice. She had Lisi bent over the coping of the wall above the mill-race, and she soaked that flame hair with paraffin, and combed it out, and I well remember the lice falling into the water and being snatched away by the stream. Then she stripped the girl's clothes, lit a fire under the wall-oven and put them inside.

Of course, like every other little animal that has found affection, Lisi Bach came for more, and she practically lived at our house after that, following my mother like a dog's tail when she was baking and churning and feeding the calves. She wanted to try her hand at all the chores, and one evening, she even went with her round the village to take the farm butter in the big basket.

I've discovered that there are some strange coincidences that cross your path sometimes, and when you are able to look at them from the perspective of time, say what you like, there seems to be some significance attached to them. On exactly the same Palm Sunday that Lisi Bach arrived, something singular happened in our lives too.

It was a fine Spring morning. The sun was drawing out the hearty aroma of the newly awakened earth. The peewits were skimming over the marshes and calling three loaves for a penny. Mother had gone to church over the Caerau Mawr leaving my father and me in the living kitchen to look after the dinner. I was sitting on the old oak settle with my head in some book, and he was by the wall-oven in the high armchair reading *John Bull*. It had a wide circulation then, weekly, but it didn't enhance your reputation to be caught reading it on Sunday. There was a gorse branch sticking out of the fire-hole under the oven, and as it was being devoured my father kicked it further in with his foot. The back door was open, and little breezes brought the peals of the church bell into the lobby now and again, and just then, what came out of that very place but a large brown dog. He didn't hesitate either, but went straight under the table, turned to follow his tail once or twice, and dropped down into a neat curl.

I drew my legs to me straightaway, because he looked to be a fierce old brute, and that bit of black that ran down his snout didn't make him appear any safer. But I need not have worried. He was asleep in no time, and my father looked at me, and we both looked at the dog in wonderment, but we let him be.

When Mother arrived from Morning Prayer, she was aghast to see such a hound under the table, because the dogs were never allowed into the house, but she was persuaded not to disturb him in case he turned nasty all of a sudden and started to chew us. And sleep he did until mid-afternoon, and when he at last awoke you never saw a milder being, but it was obvious by then that he was hungry.

My father had slaughtered a barren cow just then, and he had her hanging from a beam in the Big Barn. We 'ticed him there and cut him a piece of spare rib, and he was devouring it as if food was going to disappear from the face of the earth.

After that, my father made enquiries about the dog up and down the parish, but not a single shepherd nor gamekeeper knew anything about him, so he stayed, and we called him Gel, in a period when all the dogs were Gelert and all the cats were Twm. He had shown by then that mildness was only one side of his nature. He was the very best at turning awkward steers and sending them the way they ought to go, and he was boss of the bull too, who could be a handful in August. He would come with us to drive cattle to Anglesey over Telford's Bridge, and later we discovered that he could turn a coursing hare as well as any greyhound. He was never tied or shut in. He slept in the Big Barn on a shoulder of hay, and he was there one stormy night in winter guarding a score of fat geese. In the early hours we heard a fight going on in the Dead Marsh. It was too rough to go out, and in the morning the geese were scattered to the four points and some were mauled and there was blood on the dog's neck. He had evidently foiled some otters that came up the peat ditches to forage in the storms.

But the most wonderful thing was his relationship with Lisi Bach. They had taken to each other like *Deian* and *Loli*. Where one was, the other was bound to be, and nobody would dare touch Lisi when Gel was about; he used to accompany her all the way to the far kissing gate when she went home, and he ran to meet her when she came the other way, and once when he went with her to Llanbabo, he chewed Will, Llwynpiod's dog on the way, for looking crossways at her. Mother kept saying that it was as if the two knew the world had rejected them.

But then Lisi Bach fell ill; so ill in fact that it was evident that there was something far worse the matter with her than a mere child's ailment, and when Siani sent for Doctor Felinheli at last, he said that it was water on the brain which she'd got no doubt from those old rats. I remember going to see her with my mother, where she lay in the low bedchamber, hot and tossing in the iron bed she shared with Siani, and the first thing she asked was: "Where's Gel?" One day we took him with us, and her face was transfigured when the old dog put his paw on the bed alongside her hand, but we had a job to bring him away as if he was sensing even then how things were going to be, because it was obvious that there was not going to be a recovery for Lisi Bach. She had begun to fleer her lips and growl like a dog herself.

It was harvest-time then: sun and wind; and a gang of men had come one moonlight night to mow the Bryndu Mawr, and my father was with them. The quarrymen thought nothing of working all night then and going straight to the rock-face in the morning.

It wasn't everyone who could cut corn with a scythe and lay it in swathes. You had to start the sweep from the edge of the standing corn and bring it all cleanly to your onside until the grain and the straw were all pointing in one direction so as to facilitate the work of those who came behind to gather and bind the sheaves. I've even seen some tie a willow wand in a bow on the snead to make it easier.

That night, I'd been allowed to stay up to keep my mother company to take the men their food. We were approaching the field with the butter basket between us, and Gel was trotting in front. We could see the mowers, all in a line, swinging to rhythm, and my father was leading them on the outside. Now and again the moonlight flashed on a blade. Just as we were going through the gate, a rabbit sprang from under a stook and bolted for the shelter of the standing corn. Of course the dog could not resist a chase. The rabbit jumped into the corn in front of my father's scythe, and just as he was throwing it for a sweep, the dog arrived full-pelt, and the point of the blade went into his chest. He let out a heart-rending cry all over the night, and when Mother and I got alongside, he was stone dead on the blade.

We didn't know what to do or say, and my father must have felt like Prince Llewelyn when he killed that other Gelert by mistake. All the men put down their scythes, and my father carried the dog aside and put him down on some sheaves. The moon had gone past her arc and was hanging over the Caerau Mawr ready to drop into the Sea of Matholwch. Everybody had lost his appetite and one of the men drew out his watch. It was dead on three in the morning; a time when all life is at an ebb.

My mother had promised to go and sit up with Lisi Bach part of the night. She put up her shawl and went. "You go too," the men told my father. "We'll finish what bit is left." And go he did and me with him, and he was carrying Gel in his arms, and he put him to lie on the bench in the boiler house and covered him with a sack. Then we went into the living kitchen, and my father sat in the high armchair with his hand propping his head, and he said nothing. I sat on the old settle silent and subdued, and when I suddenly remembered that was how we were when Gel came to us first of all, I let the tears flow.

Just then we heard my mother's tread on the cobbles of the little court, and there was no need to ask why she was back so soon. When she came into the living kitchen she stood in the middle of the floor and took her shawl off very slowly.

"It's come to the end with Lisi Bach," she said at last. "She'd gone just before I got there," and then she folded the shawl and laid it on the side. "About three it was," she said again. "That's what Siani said."

My father raised his head to look at Mother, and she was looking at him in the most peculiar way, but they spoke not a word.

THE BIG WATER

The motive power at the old farm was shared between the horses and the water-wheel: things animate and inanimate as Mr Morgan Jones the parson intoned at Evensong. Consequently, these two sources of energy had to be looked after with care and nursed continually.

The water-wheel was suspended in a deep pit; its shafts on the one hand, went through the wall into the dairy to turn the thirty gallon churn on Mondays and Fridays, and on the other; to the engine house and a large pulley, which in turn drove the pulper and the chaff-cutter in the winter when the cattle had to be fed indoors.

The wheel had a wide diameter and the race was brought in by a wooden chute hanging above, so that the water, not only filled the spoons, but struck them as well with the force of gravity, thus generating more waft, so my father maintained, than the flour miller's wheel which dipped its spoons permanently in the Rhythallt river and had to be in perpetual motion.

When the spoons had reached the bottom of their turn, they spilled the water into a course that went right underneath the fold-yard like a tunnel, and emptied into the peat ditch that ran through the Dead Marsh which was the animals' graveyard. You could dig a hole large enough for anything in the Dead Marsh inside twenty minutes without a pick. The peat was moist and soft like cheese, and it came away on the spade in tidy cubes, and in no time it consumed everything. That's why for one thing, there are no traces of the old Celts who lived in the Iron Age fort above the marshes, and who grew their ancient barley in the bottoms. And at the last trump, they, and all those things we put in the peat, will be hard put to get their bones together to muster for the roll. Cows and horses, dogs and cats, and some poultry, even an Angora rabbit went into the Dead Marsh. The larger beasts had to be dragged with a swingle-tree behind the horses from wherever it was that they had expired. It was the most unprofitable labour on the land, and it was always done, like body-snatching, in the night. There was never a daytime funeral because it was considered bad husbandry to have an animal die when a man's prosperity was measured by the number of heads he had on the hoof. But killing old cows, out of milk and breath, for the dogs, was acceptable — even sending them to Belle Vue to feed the lions.

There were always some peat cubes lying loose on the surface after the burials, and in the long summers they would dry to the texture of shag. They were thrown to the far wall of the coal-house and burnt on winter evenings, while we played on the ring board or mended harness. They would smoulder like cigar ends and sustain a lazy fire for hours.

The old people must have dug for peat in large quantities on the marshes. There were large hags that filled with water after the storms, and on them the wild ducks lived and swayed at anchor under the moon. They nested on the islets, and you could wade out and get eggs for frying if the otters had not been there before you.

The churning-pond higher up was dug out of the same peat. There was a yard of water in it all year round, and when the story of Jane Owen, who ran off to drown herself in the middle of baking bread, was told it was supposed to be bottomless, and that in one respect was true because its bed was like porridge, and once it wrapped itself round your ankles, it wouldn't let go in a hurry.

It was fed by a stream which came all the way from the Jubilee Mountain, and on its journey it had turned other wheels, and unwittingly done favours, which users nearer the estuary chose to forget in order to retain their bliss. Near the corner of the pond by the overflow there was a floodgate with a T-handle at the end of a perforated bar, and it moved up and down on its slides like a sash-window. The bar could be pegged to any opening like a throttle and the flow regulated like a three-speed gear. Small Water was the notch for the churning so that the wheel turned irregularly to get the wings inside the churn to slap the milk instead of mixing it, Medium for the pulper, and for the chaff cutting — the Big Water.

I often had a race with the Big Water as it sped along the leat to the chute, like a bore on a tidal river. It swept everything before it as it curled round the hawthorn roots and under the stone bridge which took the cartroad over the marshes. It was a weekly wonder to all beholders, that is, except Lord Roberts.

Lord Roberts was the rooster who was the governor of the fold-yard in the absence of the sheepdogs. He was a cat chaser too, and as red in wattle and feather as any that came out of Rhode Island. He had spurs like a hussar, their length proving that he had survived many Christmas pogroms, and was likely only to fade away like his namesake, so popular then, whose picture hung on the wall in the living kitchen; the picture which shows him at his desk talking to the little fair-haired girl, the whole atmosphere implying that this was just the thing he was accustomed to do in between slicing Boers with the yeomanry at Bloemfontein.

After treading one or two hens to start the day, Lord Roberts would stride along the banks of the leat, one foot occasionally pausing in mid-air. He would stand by the shallows watching the minnows, jerking his head from side to side, but I think there was an element of narcissism in it too, because the clear water reflected earth and sky in their purest tones.

At dusk he would be the last to retire into the hen-house that had once been a stable. There was a manger with a slate edge still left high in the far corner, and there he perched, above the rest, like a preacher in his pulpit, ready for his early clarion. When we went to shut the hens at night and count them, he would still be awake, jerking his great comb and blinking in the lantern light.

But he never extended his patrol as far as the churning-pond, and that was just as well, because on sailing days, I couldn't do with any distractions, having my hands full, what with being captain, crew, *and* harbour-master of the floodgate and all its approaches; even to the far bank and beyond the rim of the marshes, to the shores of spice and those islands under the wind.

I had a little tin sailing-boat with a deep keel, and she tacked into the south-westerlies in tight arcs, but always stood for the far shore, and there, she ran into the long round rushes, whose heavy seed-heads bent them down like fishing-rods into the water. By accident, I discovered that they invariably acted as springs to push the little boat out again, and she would come about and homeward-bound. But some crews took longer than others to turn her about, and some couldn't manage it at all. Those I instantly dismissed. Such is the advantage of being sole owner of the line.

She had to be recovered then from that foreign port, and at such times, fantasy became mixed with perilous fact. The pond was ringed by a series of swinging bogs and quags that undulated under the slightest tread. They were deceptively covered with bog cotton and white moss, and there the cranberries grew. In the Spring, when the sun began to touch both sides of the hedges, the rims of the quags, being moist, were the first to sprout green grass. Cattle newly released after months in the shippons on a diet of dry hay, would be drawn to the swinging bogs, and many, like Carver Doone, disappeared without funerals. But there were solid tussocks in between, and if you knew the ground and were agile enough, you could cross the swinging bogs for a wager. But the thought now chills the blood, and I still maintain that Huckleberry Finn was a far worse insurance risk than the city child.

Then the day came when I was told to go myself and release the Big Water. It would have been undignified to race the bore. I restrained the urge and walked down the cartroad with control and authority like my father did, and when I reached the engine house, the race had arrived before me. It was rushing through the trap at the bottom of the chute, spilling on to the broad slate pillar that straddled the pit where I stood to have my evening shower.

The wheel was controlled by the trap. When it was pulled shut by an overhead wire the water flowed into the spoons. But it was a poor form of clutch. Even with the water diverted, the wheel, driven by its own momentum, would still revolve, and if your hand was caught in the rollers as you fed the chaff-cutter, it could be drawn into the orbit of the knives and the arm sliced like a salad cucumber right up to the elbow before anyone could intervene.

My father however, like the miller, so long used to the operation, could tell by the mere sound of the water and the cogs how things were going, and so well did he attend to the machinery, that apart from a snapping belt now and again, I can only remember one mishap with the water-wheel in all those years at the old farm.

He was chaff cutting under full power when he noticed that the wheel was 'lolloping' as they used to say when a car wheel had a flat tyre, and it was drowning, and no wonder: the pit was full of water like a bathtub and it was creeping into the engine house under the big pulley. He threw the trap, and he was on his way to shut the floodgate when he noticed water spouting out of the fold-yard. Cariad Yw happened to be about, and they both started to dig downstream of the spout, and there, stuck in the culvert, obstructing the flow, was Lord Roberts, and he looked completely done for. His wattles were pale, his comb flaccid, and the side veils were drawn over his eyes.

Cariad Yw, with the poacher's instincts, was for plucking and drawing him straightaway, but my father wouldn't hear of it. He took him to the cart-house and left him in the wheelbarrow until the night. I was told about it when I came from school, but I didn't go to see him. I knew that I would have to go to his funeral in the Dead Marsh; and that would be ordeal enough, and indeed, we all dreaded the coming of the dusk. We sat in the living kitchen waiting for the end of the October twilight, and Mother had the big linseed jug out on the fender, warm and sweet, and she'd put some extra liquorice in it too. She filled and refilled the cups, but nobody wanted any tea.

There wasn't much talk either. My father said once, as a balm to the general guilt,

"He must have gone over the wheel a couple or three times. Stood too near the bank I doubt, busybodying — got snatched into the race."

When the shades were gathering in the little lobby, Mother said to me:

"Better go shut the hens." And then: "There will be one less remember."

I took the storm-lantern across the fold-yard, and when I was passing the cart-house I didn't even turn my head. But when I got to the hen-house and held the lantern high, I didn't even stay to count. I fled back to the house.

"He's there!" I shouted. "He's there on the manger! Come and see. He's all right."

And come they did with what gallop was left in them. There was Lord Roberts, stooped a bit, still damp and with his tail feathers in disarray, perched on the edge of the manger.

"I'm damned! Well I'm damned!" was all my father could say, and that in front of Mother, but she was too astounded to notice.

It was only when we were back in the living kitchen passing our cups for one more swallow of linseed brew before the evening milking, that she said:

"We'll have to watch that old bird, or next thing, he'll be trying his luck on the big wheel at Menai Bridge Fair!"

COCK UP!

The Squire came up to the marshes to shoot twice a year as a rule. Once in November, and then he brought a larger party nearer Christmas. He was a tall man of good bearing, but it was common knowledge that he couldn't hit a haystack in an archway. All the same he had his virtues, which, according to those who are still left, were superior to the talents of some they have to deal with today.

We were given notice of his coming a few days beforehand. The gamekeeper would call at the old farm with a bundle of larch branches on his back, and he would ask us not to let the livestock stray far from the steading on that day. Then he would take his bundle of larch branches to the Dead Marsh and push them into frames that he had erected at our end, alongside the ditch, so that they formed hides for the 'guns' to shelter out of sight of the birds.

Mid-morning on the appointed day, the shooters, or the gentry as my mother — who had served them so long — called them, would arrive in their brakes in the Top Lane, and walk down the fields to the butts. They each had two guns, and a loader who followed like a dog's tail. His job was to carry the spare gun and load it and pass it back, but as far as marksmanship was concerned they were mostly in the same class as their host. If you got one in ten with a good enough eye to bring down a high flying duck cleanly, you had a man worth watching.

There would be one or two women amongst them too, with long skirts and 'Robin Hood' hats, and they usually set up shop on their own, sitting on their shooting-sticks, wasting good powder, perforating the clouds. And one I well remember took out a keeper's eye with a stray pellet.

A lorry would then take another crew and set them down like a gang of convicts at the opposite end by Rhydau Covert. They were boys from Felinheli mostly, bought for the day with a couple of shillings and a pint of beer to walk in line with sticks and cudgels across the marshes, setting up as much clamour as they could to drive the birds in the direction of the guns. It was a day out for them too; a change from holding up street-corners, and it gave them the opportunity at the same time of finding out how the inhabitants at the other end of the parish survived.

It was a big day for us too of course, bearing in mind that we only saw a cow and a few crows and John the Post from one Sunday to the next. It was at our house that they had their lunch I remember, and Mother would have kindled a fire under the wall-oven first thing, and she had a roarer going in the big grate in the front room too, and the hot water fountain alongside; the one with the big brass spigot would be steadily simmering. The harvest-home table would be dragged out into the centre, and laid all ready with the company dishes from the glass cupboard, and that, the sideboard and the brass faced grandfather clock would be shining like Waterford crystal.

But the spit and polish was not all confined to the house. The little court was brushed and a bucket of water thrown over the slates; even the foot scraper near the door was scrubbed, and the manure heap in the yard squared up and patted with the back of a shovel until it looked like an overdone loaf of *bara brith*. Even the plough-team, confined to the stables for the day, did not escape. They were curried and combed until they shone like August apples, and their tails and manes plaited and cockaded fit for the Three Counties Show.

The work on the land went to pot for the whole day. My father put on a clean collar and wore his stud, as if he was going pig killing or to a farm sale, and he scrubbed the dung off his leggings and brushed 'Cherry Blossom' into them the night before. Then we would be sitting on the granary-loft steps, as if we had paid ten round guineas for our seats. We could hear the boys shouting 'snipe' or 'cock up' as the birds rose from under their feet, and one or two old campaigners would fly cross-ways over their heads and survive for another year; but everyone blasted away at the rest as if they were making a desperate last stand against savages. We could hear the spent pellets dropping like hail on the roof of the Big Barn, and once we caught a shower ourselves.

At the same time, we kept a weather-eye for winged birds and those that fell far off where those old retrievers couldn't always find them, and at the day's end when the coast was clear, we strolled down to look for them, and sometimes we were lucky.

There was one occasion I remember especially well. It was when they came up on the eleventh of November, and a grand day it was too for shooting; light frost, sun and still, clear air. On that date, at the eleventh hour, when the guns finally shut their mouths on the Western Front and brought the carnage to a halt, it was the custom for everyone to stop whatever he was doing, and stand bareheaded for two minutes as a sign of respect for all those other boys whose names are listed on the little cenotaphs up and down the parishes. Everybody did it, regardless of class or creed.

We were on the steps as usual watching the shooting gang, and they were halfway across the Dead Marsh when it struck eleven, and we stood and bared our heads. "What will these do now?" asked my father. "Will they remember?" And just then a whistle blew and all the men doffed their hats and stood to attention in the middle of the marsh in the winter sun.

There are some small things that stick in a man's mind.

After beating the marsh, the keepers would collect the game and carry them on poles like onion men, and to get some of the birds they had to wade out up to their waists in the peat hags. Once an old gent stepped into the ditch and disappeared leaving his hat floating on top. I've seen those keepers too carrying the women over wet places like pack-mules.

Everybody would come up to the yard then, and the gentry would go into the house, while the rest lit a fire outside in the yard and suspended a cauldron above it from a tripod. Then the boys and the keepers would go into the shippon with their sandwiches and sit on the edge of the mangers, and I was running errands and fetching and carrying, and gratefully receiving pennies and sixpences from left and right to set me upon the road to further wealth. It was difficult at the time to decide whether the shippon or the front room was the best place to be to make a fortune.

In the meantime my mother would be waiting on in the front room, and bandying tattle and pouring out, and it was all food and drink for her in another way, because it gave her a brief chance of reliving all those years she had spent in service in the big houses, and she knew all the moves and the anticipations. Old Siani more often than not would arrive then in her sealskin coat; the one she kept for occasions. She would be pottering about the wall-oven, pushing more faggots underneath, or watching the mince pies, and the treat of the day for her was to be allowed to take a plateful to the front room, and exchange pleasantries with the 'little boy' as she called the Squire. She judged the social standing of the rest by the way they cleaned their boots in the scraper, and the same old custom would be observed year in and out.

The guns (Hollands to the last barrel) would be piled against the *spens* door in the lobby, and Mother, as she passed, would be sure to ask: "Are they safe, Sir Michael?"

"Perfectly, Mrs Williams. They've all been broken."

To begin with I couldn't understand how they could all be so careless as to break such nice guns.

After seeing that everything was well outside, my father would appear in the front room, and the Squire would be duty-bound to ask about the activities on the land, the yields and the livestock. Then someone would notice the war medals in the glass cupboard and ask whose they were, and that would give my father the opportunity of telling them about my uncle who was killed with the Australians on the Somme, taking great care at the same time to avoid mentioning that the Squire's grandfather had been responsible for sending him away in the first place for poaching pheasants.

Then my mother would bring out the gold hunter that belonged to her brother, Rolant, who was killed in the Dinorwig Quarries at fifteen when a bogey went over the tips. After making sure that the whole company were now aware that we had contributed in blood and money towards the preservation of the *status quo*, the conversation would be steered in the direction of more general subjects, and someone else would invariably

99

notice the single barrel alongside the clock and marvel at its length. Then my father would be off again giving the case history: how it had been the standard rifle of the Belgians in the war, and that its bore had been changed, and how he had bought it at an auction for thirty shillings, and that it didn't really matter that it had lost its bead, because it had a tendency to carry low in any case, and this and that, whilst all the time he was holding his breath lest someone should be so unwise as to ask what he used it for.

The ladies too were just as chatty, and some tried to draw Mother into telling about her days in service, and who she was with and all sorts, but she usually kept her corner pretty well with the best of them.

Once a French girl came, with dark hair and a retroussé nose, and darker eyes, shining so bright that you could practically shave in them. It was Siani who told me about her as soon as I came in from the yard, because she was — of all the things in the whole world — smoking mind you, and that with a long holder too. When I went in, tongue-tied and awkward, there she was, sitting on the old sofa by the window, puffing away and looking just like those *de Reskes* adverts. She asked me straight away to sit beside her, and there we were exchanging Welsh and French nouns and idioms and having great fun. In a very short time I had become her veritable slave and wishing she could stay the whole day; but go she had to, and for a long time after I was hoping that she would come again, but she never did.

By the time they had drained their glasses and gone out again, the horse-drawn dray, carrying the game, would have arrived. It was covered with a tarpaulin, looking for all the world like a Wild West waggon, and dead birds and animals of all kinds were hanging inside. It was attended by an old-timer whose luck was better than most, for when everyone had gone to the Foel for the afternoon after the grouse, he would be asked into the house to clear the mince-pies and have a chat with Siani about the long ago time, and of how things were not quite the same as they used to be. But Mother always cautioned him about the port, in case he hit a gate-post and capsized the whole morning's work.

At dusk, when Siani was on her way home with her basket full of tarts and *bara brith*, I would go down to the Dead Marsh to collect the empty cartridge cases, and they were of a variety of colours, and smelt of cordite. I would fill my pockets, and in the long dark evenings I would stand them in a row on top of the door in the living kitchen and knock them over with my pop-gun and cork bullet. Those hours unwittingly served to give me a fair eye by the time I was ready to carry the old Belgian, and other guns in a later war, and hold them straight. But whenever I fire it now and smell the powder, I always think of shooting days, and the guests in the shippon and the front room at the old farm, long ago.

STONES AND SNOOKERS

In May, the slopes of the Elidir Mountain were emerald green. The wintering ewes had returned from the floor of the parish and by degrees were receding up the *ffridd* with their lambs to their summer habitat. The swallows were already making their inverted mud huts under the beams in the Big Barn. On the banks of the Rhythallt river the pink clover was sickly sweet.

There was activity in the village too. Will Green's wife had hung her 'Refreshments' sign on the gate, and Mr Thomas, chemist, had brought his revolving postcard stand out on the pavement. Will Maethlon Jones, grocer, had discovered he didn't have the nerve to open for tobacco and sweets on Sundays, and Ifan Parry, the Bard, had delivered his edict from his armchair by the coke stove in his billiard and shaving-saloon in Gold Terrace: There were too many foreigners coming to spoil the as yet unmarred beauty of the hills.

There were four houses in Gold Terrace and Ifan Parry owned them all. He had been with the Royal Welch fighting Johnny Turk on the beaches of Gallipoli, and later, had fought him in the desert with Colonel Lawrence and his camels. After that, he had gone West and made his fortune in the mines of Montana, and then he had come home and bought property. He thought he could live tidily as a lenient landlord, but values had fallen like soot in the night, so in order to be able to have his cigar after supper, he had knocked the two end-houses into one and made a billiard saloon.

I remember that night I went down for a frame and a trim. He always had a soft spot for me ever since I won the junior chair for a poem at the Bethania eisteddfod, and he wanted to instil in me the mysteries of the four and twenty measures, for he was no mean poet himself; having been barred from competing in several parishes because he had that many chairs he didn't know where to put them. He was known locally as the Bard, and cherished as such, although old Siani was dead against him: 'because he took the boys' money with his little coloured balls.' Will Maethlon Jones had even called him a crank, and that over the counter, when he took back a quarter of ham saying that it was underweight. And I must say myself that he could be peculiar; to an extent I was to discover on that evening in May.

On my way, I stopped for a moment to watch the water weeping down the moss into the quarry pit. It was quiet in the village. The sun had dropped below the Marconi Mountain and there was a soft pink afterglow. The houses were in the shadow and were clinging to the slope to save themselves sliding into the lake over which the swallows were collecting gnats.

Both tables were on the go that night, and there was the hum of after work conversation and the click of ivory. The aroma of Amlwch tobacco mingled with the sweet smell of the shaving-soap and the brilliantine. The big lampshades hung low over the tables, and the grey smoke curled upwards over their edges like wraiths in the night.

Ifan Parry was haircutting in the far corner by the window. When he heard the latch he paused, holding the open scissors in mid-air and lowering his leonine head, the better to see over his gold-rimmed glasses. Will Green was in the chair, and the Bard was holding forth on a touchy subject, for he had embraced nationalism, and he went at night to dab his slogans on the rocks with his white-wash brush. But Will was saying nothing. His wife was in the bed and breakfast business, and everyone knew who wore the trousers. He was holding his chin askew out of the way of a cue-butt, held by a youth who had his ball on the cush.

After I'd been in the chair and downed a frame of snooker, the men gradually drifted away to have their eight hours before pitting their skills against the rock-face in the morning. Ifan Parry began to brush the tables and cover them with the cloths, and I helped him with the corners. He was complaining about the quarry boys leaning over the baize in their work clothes. I've often imagined his last words being quoted amongst those of the famous: 'Gentlemen — please use the rests.'

He riddled the fire in the coke stove which heated the kettle for the shaving-water, and he spat into the ash-pit. "Coming up for a minute?" he asked.

I wasn't keen, and we had a friendly exchange, but he won. I followed him upstairs to his little bachelor's flat. The living-room was choked with bookcases, and there was a grandfather clock with a blue ship rocking above its face. The heavy leaf table was covered with a thick brown cloth with long tassels hanging on its edges, and on it were piled more books and manuscripts, and the Mabinogion, and the Imperial Gazetteer. Will Green's wife came to clean three times a week, and for that Ifan Parry forgave her the rent. For her, as far as I could see, it was a bargain.

The Bard made some tea and he was uncommonly quiet, and I thought at first that the muse was upon him. Then at last he said:

"I don't feel like anything to eat, and I don't want to keep you. The truth is, I've suddenly decided to go on the Ridge. I want to see what I can do with the Arrow Stone. I'd like to have company, but I don't want anyone who will blab. Are you game?"

"What are you going to do up there?" I asked.

"Well, it's hard to explain. In any case, it would take too much time. Better you wait and see the thing done. I'm asking you to have faith in me tonight. I'll grant you that you will get to know everything at the proper time. This morning I had an impulse about the Arrow Stone. Will you come?"

After that, he would have had a job to stop me. We sat by the fire until we heard the boozers going past from the Big Inn, and then Ifan Parry put on his black coat and grey muffer. "We'll go seperately," he said. "You first. Wait for me at the bridge."

I didn't see anyone on the way, but I heard a car going down the High Street. It must have been Doctor Roberts going to minister at a sick bedside, blissfully unaware of healthier souls out on darker errands.

It was a starry night. When the Bard arrived at last, we leaned on the bridge parapet for a while, for it wasn't a job to be rushed. The river slid underneath like a blade going into a sheath and down the valley it roared faintly as it rolled over the round stones, like grain going down a chute. Then we crossed the water-meadow that led on to the rising ground of the Blue Ridge which was obnly a dark blob in front. You would never dream that in daylight you could see the profile of a woman on it. Her hair is thick and combed in a curve to the nape of her neck, and she is looking down towards the sea as if expecting someone from a distant land. I've always thought that she is a sad woman, but she is young, although the age of the rocks that form her chin and nose and forehead can be counted in aeons. And I've always thought too that I ought to know her.

Ifan Parry walked in front up the slope. He was a good scrambler and strong. I followed the dark figure and recollected the stories he had told me about Gallipoli, Colonel Lawrence and his camels, and the Montana mines. And now, I was going to share an actual experience with him — perhaps the strangest of all. The gloom pressed around us. In its substance there was a rich mixture of the perfumes of the May night.

If you don't know where it is, you'd never find the Arrow Stone in summer when it is covered with bracken-fronds. It is a flat stone, like a casket, and its face is marked with many runnels. Down the centre there is a deep runnel, and the others run into it like veining on a leaf. Ifan Parry used to say that the old Britons had used it as a whetstone for their arrows.

We were warm by the time we arrived at the stone. Ifan Parry stood very still. He did not speak either, he only looked down on the dark surface of the lake whose bed had been gouged by the blades of the glaciers. Then he turned and walked to the Arrow Stone. He parted the fronds and knelt down beside it on the damp earth, and rested both his hands on the slab. His broad head was bare, and the starlight shimmered very faintly on his white hair as it curved over his crown. His head was slightly inclined and his hands began to creep along the stone as his fingertips sought the runnels. Then I heard him mumble. He mumbled so much and groaned that I began to worry about him. I was afraid for one thing that he might be having a stroke, but when I moved towards him, he began to speak very clearly. He said that it was a summer's day on the Ridge. The sun was beating down hotly, and a group of men were descending the slope. They were small men, broad men I heard him say, clad in skins and they carried bows. They came straight to the stone. Then Ifan Parry said something else in an excited manner: one of the men was naked. He did not carry a bow. His wrists were bound in front of him and he was thrown on his face on to the sward.

Then Ifan Parry said that he saw three men, each in turn, kneel by the stone. They had arrows in their hands and they ran the heads along the wide runnel. It took a long time for the men to whet the arrows, and Ifan Parry lapsed again into his mumbling speech. Then suddenly he cried out very clearly again into the night: "No, don't do it! Don't do it!" And he collapsed on the stone.

I got hold of him then and pulled him off, and he was shaking violently. It was a long time before he was able to stand and walk unsteadily down towards the bridge. We went very slowly through the village, and I was glad when we arrived back at the flat, because I had been expecting to see P.C. Jenkins coming round every corner.

Ifan Parry sat in the rocking-chair. He was still shivering slightly. He rolled a cigarette and began to speak softly and modestly. He said that what I had witnessed on the Ridge was the practice of the science of Psychometry. It was wonderful to possess the power apparently; Colonel Lawrence himself had it. Yet, very often the experiences connected with it were terrifying. He had known that there was some unpleasantness connected with the Arrow Stone all along, and he had always been afraid to investigate, but he was glad he had ventured at last. He knew now what it was, but he didn't tell me any more about the little men and their arrows. He sat and smoked in his chair, gently rocking himself, and while I made some tea, he stared drowsily into the fire and began to talk of other things.

HOME KILLED OR CURED

We were more or less self-supporting at the old farm as far as food was concerned. We had milk and butter, meat and vegetables all the year round, and we took a ton of oats to the miller every autumn. A pig was killed and salted each Spring and at the back end, and its meat would be hanging in the milk-house: always available. Old barren cows were slaughtered for the dogs, and occasionally a bullock for our own use.

The pig was selected out of the litter early on, before the weaners were sold to the smallholders. It was fed on the best meal and butter-milk, and chaffed nettles were an ingredient of its feed.

When the day for the killing arrived, the slates on the engine house floor were scrubbed clean and ready, and all necessary equipment for the operation laid neatly to hand. We had a short piece of wood with a loop of cord attached to the end. The first move was to catch the pig and get the loop inside its mouth. The loop would then be twisted tightly round its snout. This implement was called a twitch. It was used on animals generally when they needed treatment, before the advent of tranquilisers.

We would then drag the pig into the engine house and stick it. The blood ran into the water-wheel pit unless my mother chose to catch it in a bucket, to make black-pudding. When the pig finally dropped, scalding water was poured on it and the bristles scraped off. Then my father would cut a notch between the bone and the tendon of the hindlegs and insert the ends of a piece of notched wood, called a *cambran*, a couple of feet in length, above the trotters. A ladder was then placed against the wall and the carcass tied to one of the rungs. It was easy then to split the belly and allow the intestines to drop into a tub. Some of the guts were thrown to the dogs, after Mother had selected the best casings for the black-puddings.

The pig was then taken on to the slate slab in the milk-house where it was cut into flitches and decapitated. The brains were removed from the head, before the latter was boiled and pickled into brawn. The hams were cut away and salted. They were put into muslin bags which Mother had prepared, and hung.

All kinds of operations were performed on sick animals too, and remedies prescribed. It is still a mystery to me how those Yorkshire vets, whose activities during the same period have been so much publicised, ever made a living. Their clients must have either been more prosperous, or less capable than their counterparts amongst the yeomen who lived on the floor of Llanddeiniolen parish in my time. To have a vet enter a farmyard was an admission of impracticability and bad husbandry, not to mention the expense. I don't remember any being summoned to the old farm. If the condition of a sick animal had deteriorated beyond the ministrations of my father and two other men, recognised as country animal farriers in their own rights, then it was futile to call for further advice, pay for it, and in addition, lose the animal.

The methods and the medications would seem outlandish today, even barbaric, but they were often effective. Standard tools and instruments were kept to deal with most common maladies. There was always a cow horn hanging on the shippon wall to administer medicine through the mouth. There was a supply of pitch for plastering broken legs and horns. There were tongs for paring hooves; a small, circular knife to knock into the abdomens of cows swelling with the wind; needles of many varieties to sew cows with prolapse or the ejection of the womb after calving; ropes and tackle to pull out cross-grained calves, or for lifting animals bodily off the floor, and a short, pointed poker from the house for ringing bulls.

On the window-ledges there was a dispensary of liniment bottles and shag tobacco for horses with colds, and ribbed bottles of blue glass containing the panacea of the times for man and beast: Morus Ifans' Oil. They were encased in strands of cobwebs, which were sometimes used to staunch blood.

Poultry also was just as prone to its own peculiar accidents and discomforts. It was common in the spring to see chickens hobbling about with leg splints. Other birds, especially roosters, became crop-bound. They were opened with razors and the blockage removed.

Young chicks by the dozen were prone to a condition known as 'gape'. Their beaks were continually yawning as they fought for breath. They picked up a bug in the grasses which developed into a thread-worm in the windpipe, obstructing the air passage.

There were three methods of removing the thread-worm, and they were all drastic: my father whittled a quill until there was only a tuft of feather left at the end. He would hold the bird's beak open and push the quill down the windpipe and withdraw it with a sharp twist. Very often the worm would come out with the quill.

Another way was to throw green leaves on the fire to make smoke, and hold the chick's head in it until it literally choked. This induced it to sneeze and expel the worm.

The last resort however was the carbolic fume treatment. We had a small ammunition chest with a close-fitting lid. The inside was divided into two compartments by a piece of wire-netting. Half-a-dozen afflicted chicks were placed in one half, and a hot brick in the other. Carbolic acid was then poured onto the brick, which gave off thick choking fumes, and the lid of the chest was shut. The chicks remained in that atmosphere until their scratching and squawking ceased. The lid was then opened and the chest tipped on its side. Most of the occupants would bolt and scatter, sneezing as they went. For others the ordeal was too much.

There was one man however who was tolerated in the farmyard to operate upon animals because his services were indispensable. He was Thomas Jones, the gelder, who lived in Dwyran on the west side of Anglesey, from which place he came on his push-bike over Telford's Bridge on to the mainland and the extremities of Caernarfonshire to ply his exacting trade.

He carried his instruments in a box tied to the back of the bike: knives, tongs, and pincers, needles and cauterising iron, and a tool like a guillotine, for docking tails. He came at all seasons, daunted neither by wayside dangers nor darkness, for although not of large proportions, he could hold his corner pretty well with tongue and fist, and his cycling exertions never impaired the steadiness of his hand. With him he brought tales and news from the other side of the river.

He told us once of a man from Brynsiencyn whose pride was his garden and his apple-tree, but he was plagued with crows by the dozen. All attempts at repelling them had been futile. They would fly off a short distance and recongregate in the branches of the apple-tree, and from there they mocked him with their raucous cries.

Then, one evening, he plastered the tree with bird-lime, and the following morning, seeing the birds trapped in the branches, he took a bag, meaning to pick them like apples. But at his approach, the crows took off in one body, uprooting the tree and taking it with them. The last he saw of either was crossing the river for the mainland...

Thomas Jones was also an exponent of sleight-of-hand with cards and matches, and he kept us enthralled round the milk-house table with tricks of the 'now you see it — now you don't' variety. Cards disappeared to come to light again in the most unlikely corners. Lighted cigarettes were swallowed and made to reappear from people's ear-holes and armpits, but all that happened after the completion of the serious work.

The animals that needed his attention would have been brought together in the early morning, and although he went to two or three other farms during the day, he was never in any hurry. We began with the smaller fry and worked upwards. The piglets were the first patients. My work was catching them by the hindlegs and holding them upside down between my thighs while they were cut. Then we moved to the yearling cattle. They had to be thrown, and that was easiest done by holding on to the offside ear with the arm thrown over the neck from behind, and then inserting thumb and fingers of the free hand in the nostrils, depriving them of air. Then it was a question of hanging on and bearing down on the side of the neck. Some fell quickly, others would carry you round like a shopping basket before giving up.

Bulls and stallions were another matter. They had to be twitched with the stick and loop, but all these operations ended satisfactorily for man and beast. Colts and fillies had their tails docked with the guillotine.

Because I was strong then and quick-footed, I was lent to

Thomas Jones at his request to be his apprentice for the day at the other farms. My work was to heat the iron in the kitchen fire and run with it red-hot when it was called for. The gelder then would cauterise the severed veins. But no one I knew ever lost an animal after the ministrations of Thomas Jones, and what strikes me now as remarkable about this primitive surgery, was the absence of gore in any quantity. As a matter of fact, he selected the best testicles to take to an old lady in Dwyran who was partial to them fried with new potatoes.

But for home-devised veterinary ingenuity, the case I best remember is that of a large sow with a tumour in its gullet which stopped it feeding.

Thomas Jones's visit had been arranged to coincide with that of a neighbour who had come to help my father kill or cure the animal. there were no means of sedation then. They had to put two twitches on the sow, and that operation alone was like fighting a crocodile. When they eventually got its mouth open, they inserted a board behind its fangs to stop it snapping them shut. In the centre of the board they had bored a hole wide enough to take a broomstick, at the end of which they had securely tied the pig-sticking knife. My father was then able to slice off the growth slowly without fear of going into the jugular. The sow, even then, nearly bled its life away, but happily it survived to suckle several more litters.

It was pure irony of course that these animals were cossetted to survive, only to be slaughtered later, for our own survival.

SMALL MERCIES

I once worked for a firm of auctioneers in North Wales, and my duties took me up and down the country, the length of the Llŷn Peninsula and the whole of Anglesey.

It was tiresome work but interesting. I went to the cattle marts, the weekly sales, the furniture auctions in private houses, and, at the back end, to dispersal sales in the farms and the smallholdings. These were somehow more personal events, because for the most part they involved some tragedy or misfortune: a death, failure, or some disability to carry on.

I went one autumn about Fair time to a small farm on the East coast of Anglesey where those steep rocks plunge right down to the sea. It was a windy day, and when I arrived with the auctioneer and saw what had to be gone through, I didn't look forward to the task one bit. From what I could see we would be still at it at dusk. I was right: we had to use a couple of storm-lanterns to sell the furniture.

When the selling was over the auctioneer usually disappeared, leaving me to deal with the accounts of the buyers and the vendors, but there was always somebody about to make a meal and a cup of tea, which made all the difference when the working-day was extended into the evening.

But in that particular place there were no refreshments. When I came to think of it, there was no one in attendance at all. Throughout the day, I only spoke to one person who knew anything about the property. She was a wild looking woman who was dashing hither and thither with a bundle of keys in her fist. She told me that the farm had belonged to a bachelor uncle of hers, and after telling me to pull the door to before I went, she disappeared completely.

At six o' clock in the evening I was still making out the bills in a damp little parlour with dried shepherd's purse in the grate. Not a bite had passed my lips since morning, and I was dying to get done with the unfriendly spot.

At last, I got rid of the last customer. I slammed the door, startling a family of sparrows in the overhanging ivy, and crossed the yard to the cart-house where I had left the firm's old car. I had about five thousand pounds in my bag, and that had to be taken back to the office on the mainland. But then we had no worries about being mugged and robbed. Nowadays, I would not have been so happy.

The wind had gone down a bit by the evening and there was a scud of cloud driving across a high moon. All else was quiet; there seemed to be no one in the whole parish but me.

When I was just putting my foot inside the car, I heard a voice.

"Where will you go now?"

I let the car door swing shut again, and in the doorway of the cart-house I saw a form, and just then I remembered the voice. I'd heard it before, that very morning, on the field when we were selling some job-lots before starting on the implements.

The job-lots consisted mainly of useless scrap, brought to light of day after lying for many years in corners, and Tomi the Scrap usually bought them all. But that morning I noticed that a little old lady was holding against him bid for bid, and in the end, she got them, and when she came to pay me with ready cash, I had a better look at her.

She had small, boot button eyes, and a brown hat with a wide brim. She wore an old raincoat down to her ankles, brought tight round her middle with a piece of sash-cord. She had a large hawking-basket on her arm, the bottom resting on her hip-like a peddling gypsy.

Of course, she was not an oddity in rural Anglesey in those days straight after the War. People were still ageing with grace and dignity. But now, you'll hardly ever see an old lady like that. The grannies today are fancy spectacled and blue rinsed, and painted, as if they were the advance guard of a travelling circus.

"I bet you haven't had a bite all day," said the voice. "Would you like to come with me for provender?"

"I wouldn't mind," I said, just like that. After all, when you're half-starving, the Devil's soup is just as tasty as the feast of St. John.

"Come on then," she said, and out I went into the moonlight.

I followed her through the gate into the paddock. She was a smaller body than I had imagined, but she was quite agile.

"Where do you live?" I said.

"Just beyond these couple of fields."

I was walking with her alongside the high hedge and the moon was shining intermittently through the scud. I noticed that she had a tendency to busybody, and for all I knew, she might have had her mind on the contents of the bag, and on casting my mind back to the events on the field, I remembered seeing her several times on the edge of the crowd, looking towards me in the most peculiar manner. But as I said, I was hungry, and I dismissed all doubts. I asked at last:

"Did you get a bargain in the job-lot?"

"I don't know lad. I only wanted that old butter scales you see. I haven't had a proper look at it yet."

We rounded some rocks, and then I heard the sound of the sea breaking. Presently we came to a small house, guarded on three sides by outbuildings. The top of the guard door was open.

"Come in," she said and shoved the bottom open with her knee.

There was a paraffin lamp on the table with the flame turned down. The fire had been heavily banked.

She turned up the lamplight, and gave the fire a good poking until it burst into a merry blaze.

"Take off your coat," she said. "Would you like a toddy, to warm?"

"I would," I said. "What have you got?"

"Wine," she said. "But it's good. Come on and choose."

I followed her across the room through a low doorway into a

114

small dairy. She placed the lamp on a slate bench and knelt by a cupboard set in the white-washed wall.

"Come here," she said, and opened the cupboard.

I looked inside and saw a stout wooden box, and on the side was printed in large black lettering the word KRIEGSMARINE.

"Pull it out," she said.

When I did so, I saw that it contained a round dozen bottles of wine, red and white.

"Where did you get these?" I asked.

"Choose one and bring it."

I knew less about wines then than I do now, which amounts to very little, but I knew they were of German origin.

After taking out a bottle of red, I replaced the box and returned to the living room with the bottle. After the cold atmosphere of the dairy it was cosier still there, but I shan't attempt to describe its contents. I've never seen a Welsh kitchen before or since so representative of its period, and I've been in a great many. I'm sure that poorer specimens have been carted off in one piece to the Folk Museum before now.

I sat in the ingle with my wine-glass, and on the shelf above, amongst the candlesticks and the brassware I saw two photographs in silver frames. One was of a young man in seafaring clothes, the other was a middle-aged man with a heavy moustache.

The old lady was taking a clean cloth out of the table drawer, and she caught me looking at the photos.

"That was my husband," she said. "He was killed in that old Parys mine, and the other one is Robin — in the War you see — he was in the Merchant. Were you in it?"

"I was flying."

"Get away. You don't know much about the sea then?"

"Very little."

She opened the oven-door in the range and drew out a bowl of soup.

"Come to the table," she said, "while it's hot."

I took my wine-glass with me, and I started to devour the soup.

"How is it?"

"Wonderful," I said, and that was the truth, because by that time, what with the warmth without, and the wine within, my opinion of the parish and its natives generally had undergone a considerable change for the better. I forgot the discomforts of the past day, and then, a thought struck me. It wasn't just a sudden whim that had possessed the old girl to prepare all that for me and come down to look for me. This welcome had been planned well in advance.

"How do you like the wine then?"

"It's good. It warms you."

"Do you understand what it says on the bottle?"

"I'm afraid I don't. Anyway it's what's inside that counts."

"It's been here for six years you know, untouched."

"Never."

"Fact. That's the first bottle to be opened, and I'll tell you how it came here too."

She had gone to sit in the corner that I had vacated, and she was smoothing down her apron with her palm.

"One evening in the War it was," she said. "Very much like tonight, autumn, but mild. I was sitting here, exactly as I am now. I'd just been to give the cow the last feed, and was waiting for the nine o'clock news on the radio. Remember how we used to wait for the nine o'clock especially those with people in the thick of it — and your mother too, I'm sure.

Robin was on those convoys you know, bringing stuff from America. And I knew very well that those submarines were waiting for them like eels. I've heard the boys say more than once that they used to lie on the bottom for a while — just biding their time for the ships.

Anyway, here I was, alone even then, but I wasn't afraid either, you know. I was worrying too much about Robin and the boys to think overmuch about myself...

"Will you have some more soup?"

After getting me another helping, she went back to her corner. I didn't know whether she was telling the truth or not, but I didn't care very much by then. What was keeping my interest more than anything was the fact that something belonging to it had to do with me. What exactly, at the time, I had no means of telling.

"Well, the top half of the guard door was open," she said, "exactly as it is tonight, and I heard heavy footsteps on the little path. It wasn't Robin, I knew, and for a moment I thought it could be one of the boys, home from the sea, come to see how I was and to ask about Robin. They used to come quite often you see. But the next thing I saw was the head and shoulders of a man over the guard door, and he had a grey beard. He pushed the

116

door open and came in. He had a pistol in his hand and it was pointing at me. And he stood right in the middle of the floor there.

"Good evening, madam," he said, just like that.

He was dressed in seafaring clothes and a peaked cap. I knew very well that he had nothing to do with our boys, and I didn't know what to say. I half rose but sat down again.

"I'm sorry to disturb you," he said, and just then two lads, little ratings you know, rushed in, with rifles, and placed themselves one each side the door like ramrods.

"Is there anyone with you?" the man asked.

"No," I said — "not a soul."

He barked at the little lads, and off they went, one to the dairy, and the other to the loft, and by then my mind had had a chance to move a bit.

I knew they were Germans of course, and the first thing that came to my mind was that they were prisoners broken out of some camp, but seeing their guns and the way they went about their affairs, I changed my mind.

When the two ratings returned and placed themselves again each beside the doorway, the man looked at Robin's photograph and that of his father.

"Where are they?" he asked.

"Out," I said ever so quickly.

I don't know whether he believed me or not, but he put the pistol in his pocket. But something had told me that he wouldn't use it on anyone unless he was absolutely forced. He said something else to the lads, and out they went like a shot. Then he turned to me.

"I've been in a skirmish," he said, "and got the worst of it. There are a few dead, the doctor amongst them. And some are wounded — one very seriously. I shall have to leave him behind to get attention. You'll take care of him — but I need an hour's leeway — one hour remember."

Things were by then piling up so quickly on me that I became a little confused and frightened, and when you are like that the most unlikely thing comes to your mind.

"Where will you go?" I said, and I was on my feet by then.

He looked round the room. He was a comparatively young man you know, but aged before his time with his responsibility. His eyes softened, and he looked me straight in the eye.

"Home," he said. "I hope."

And just then two other sailors came in carrying a stretcher, and there was a boy lying on it, and they placed him on the table. I took a look at him — *mam bach* — there's a sight he was. His clothes were covered in blood for a start, and his arm looked as if it was half hanging off, and someone had just tied a cloth round him to keep it on. But his face, that's the funny part — was perfectly clean. A fair-haired boy he was with large blue eyes and they were full of pain.

"He's not to have a drop of anything," said the man at last. "He's hurt internally you see. But you'll have to give me an hour before you go and seek anyone. It's nine on that clock now. Don't go outside this house until ten, or we shall fire on you." He paused for a bit, then he said simply, 'Thank you', and out they all went, and I never saw them again."

"Well where had they come from?" I asked before she had the opportunity of saying anything else.

"From the bottom there somewhere, under the cliffs as far as I know. It's not very far you know, only there's some climbing to do. I've argued about it dozens of times with Robin and the boys, but none of us are any the wiser."

"What did they suggest?"

"Well, that there was a U-Boat down there somewhere that night, damaged, and they wanted to try and repair her before setting out again. Of course the biggest puzzle is why she was lying on *this* coast and not on the Atlantic side."

She was so emphatic about it all that I couldn't but by then believe her. "What happened after that?" I asked.

"Well, that is the longest hour that I spent in all my life I think. I was left on my own with that poor wounded body, and there was nothing I could do for him you see, and I expect it was just as well, because the man had told me not to give him anything. He was moaning, and sometimes mumbling something in his own language. Many a time I had thought what I would like to do to those old Germans when I read about the way they were treating people, but when one of them was at my mercy I could think of nothing but compassion.

I remember very well sticking my head over the guard door to listen but I could hear nothing. If it wasn't for that poor soul on the table, I would have had to put my finger in the fire to convince myself that it had all happened.

I was looking at that old grandfather clock every other minute, and it seemed as if it had a hundredweight of lead stuck to its pendulum. I thought once of chancing it down to the farm, guns or no. Old Ellis lived there then. But of course, the man had asked for one hour.

What did it matter about that, you may well ask. Well nothing I expect, but there you are. The soul is a complicated thing, say what you like.

"What happened then?" I asked.

"When it came a quarter to the hour I couldn't bear it any longer. I threw my shawl over my shoulders and off I went, right along that path we came on just now. I saw not a soul. But the most difficult task was to get old Ellis to understand, and I let him go down to report.

As you can imagine no one came for another hour, but when they did, there were soldiers and policemen and all kinds, and in the end they took the boy away to hospital."

She fell quiet then for a minute or two.

"He died on the way you know," she said in a bit. "I got to know later."

"Oh."

"Yes. And I've always been sorry you know that I didn't go sooner. They were only trying to frighten me by saying one hour."

"Do you think so?"

"Oh yes — I do."

"But you did what you could. It must have been terribly upsetting. Tell me though. Did you hear any more about it — the submarine?"

"Not a whisper. As a matter of fact I'd put it more or less out of my mind — that is until today."

"Oh — how do you mean?"

"I was standing in the field this morning waiting for the auction to start, and I happened to turn my head, and I saw you coming down with the auctioneer, and something caught at my breath."

"What was the matter?"

"Do you know that you are the very image of that boy who was on the table that night?"

I didn't know what to say; she had given me a wonderful meal, and I was ready to collect my traps and start for home.

"Isn't that funny?" I said at last.

She did not mention the incident again for the remainder of the time I was there, and presently I stood up and thanked her for her hospitality.

"You'll have to come across the river to see us one day," I said.

"I must," she said, thrusting the half-empty wine bottle into my hand. "Take that with you."

"Thank you," I said with my hand on top of the guard door. "But weren't you going to tell me how you came by the wine?"

"Well, of course, what came over me pray? The box was here, on the floor when I returned from the farm, but of course I'd put it away you see before anyone arrived."

"Very wise," I said.

"Wasn't I too?"

"Well good-bye now and thank you."

"Good-bye lad. Remember to come and see me again."

"I'm sure to come."

But of course, I never went. The chances are — it's too late now.

OVER THE HILLS AND FAR AWAY

I tramped the Marches once, after the Second World War, with a bag and a billy-can, begging hot water and sleeping in hayricks and workhouses. There was plenty of casual work to be had in the fields and gardens, if you felt like doing it, but I wouldn't recommend it as the ideal life to anyone, especially nowadays, and I gave it up eventually for the slightest reason.

I was in Hay on Wye one Guy Fawkes night, looking for a place to lay down my head, when I was pursued by a gang of children, who perhaps thought I was the man himself. They pelted me with rip-raps, and my railwayman's surtout, the one that served as coat and blanket, was singed on the sleeve. I was glad to escape down a side-alley, and I thumbed my way out of that place of cursed memory. Funny how one unpleasant experience puts you off some places for ever.

Before morning, I'd found a stack in a rickyard near Pershore, but I was caught there at first light, by an old-timer with a cavalry moustache. He didn't turn out to be a bad old sort however. Mind you, my kind were ten-a-penny in those days, as they are after every war and conflict: misfits, disappointed people, geniuses too some of them, that the Establishment had discarded, now that their capacities could not be used for destruction.

I was no sensation in the life of the old-timer however. He

was the owner of the steading, and later I found that he had ridden with the yeomanry in the Boer War, and in his day, it was said that he could slice ten lemons hung in a row with a sabre from the saddle of a galloping horse.

He had a caravan in the rickyard, and he made me an offer. I could live in it all winter long, provided I pruned his cider orchards. I took it up, and a more fortunate man never happened that way. The old man had taken to me: I was fed on the best oatmeal, and I had home cured bacon across my pan every other day, and he pressed his own cider-apples. You would have thought I was the prodigal, fresh from the land of the husks, and I suppose the analogy is in many ways apt.

The winter went by with driving East winds and snow-flurries which came over the flatlands from Warwick, but I was pitched in the lee of a great straw rick, which roared and crackled in the draught. On New Year's Eve I went to Huddington Court, the old Elizabethan mansion, where the Gunpowder Plot itself was hatched, hoping, as the local belief had it, to see Lady de Wyntour, gliding across the lawn in her long blue gown. But she never came.

The Spring however eventually did, bringing warm breezes from the shores of Spain to waft over the Malverns, and with them, came the gypsies, in a long procession of horse-drawn *vardos* and flat carts, down the Droitwich Road from Birmingham, (the *Kaulo Gav*, the black town, as they called it.) They worked in the fields down the Evesham Vale in families; from the oldest grandmother to the merest maid, gathering the crops as they ripened. Amongst them were the Coopers.

I had been pea-picking in their company once, and gained access to their fires after work. I've always been drawn to such people; and they to me. They told me that my colouring, being so different to theirs made me a talisman of good fortune, a charm, a living amulet, to be constantly kept within sight, and on occasions, even touched.

As in every family, there were girls, and one of those was Sinffi Cooper. She was taller than the average gypsy woman, and statuesque. When she stood completely at ease and relaxed, she resembled those old sculptures from Greece in the long ago time. On the quiet, I thought she was in love with me, as I was with her, but we wouldn't have dared carry the idea any further. She would have been banished, and I might have had a knife in my ribs.

But I went with her and the others to Worcester Fair. After

trading their horses and telling fortunes and making themselves a holy nuisance in the shops, they enticed me into the back parlour of The Old Pheasant in the Shambles and had me drink myself silly on perry. Then they took me back on the deck of a flat cart like a bundle of carrots, and Sinffi was standing with either foot astride me, driving the pony as if she was Buddug coming home from battle. They dumped me on a heap of straw in the rickyard, and when I recovered enough to take notice, the fleur-de-lys brooch I wore to remember my mother, had gone. Well what can you do? As the old yeoman said: "What do you expect with having truck with such people?"

But I was still very friendly with Sinffi. She came to the rickyard some evenings, and I had acquired an old typewriter by then, like a combine harvester, and nothing would please her more than to be allowed to tap out her name, although she was illiterate in all other respects. One evening she arrived with a hawking-basket full of peas and she sat on the step in the sunset, shelling them, and unthinking, as one is wont to do, I asked a disastrous question:

"You haven't told my fortune yet have you?"

"I can't," she said quite emphatically.

"Why not?"

"I *belong* to your fortune, brother."

"But you can't leave your people and betray your blood."

"Not on this side, brother. I can on the other. You and me will be together then. When they have burned my things, when I am old as old, I shall have gone to the Duvel, and there will be two new stars on the side of the sky. You and me will be they, brother. Our souls are the same you see."

"Do you think so Sinffi?"

"I am certain of it, brother."

I didn't see Sinffi for a week after that. The family had moved nearer to Evesham to work, but one evening her small sister came to the rickyard with a message for me, and she delivered it as if she was reciting the Litany.

"Go to the big oak in Spetchley Wood when the moon is rising tomorrow night."

Spetchley Wood was a wonderful place in the summertime. It was like walking into a green cathedral with the choir-stalls filled with wood-pigeons and blackbirds and cuckoos, singing the *Te Deum* unaccompanied all day. That night however, I had a stranger experience than I've had in any woodland since. The moon was appearing. For a summer one it was bright between the leaves. The bole of the old oak was thicker than usual, and when I peered I knew that there was someone standing against it.

"Sinffi," I said. "Is that you?"

"Don't come near me," she said.

"What do you want?"

"I've come to look at the moon."

She was wearing her long Fair dress. I leant on another tree.

"The moon is strong you know," she said again. "She is generous in giving, but much stronger in drawing. She pulls the tides."

"Who told you that?"

"She puts the bloom on apples in the night, and she draws poison from wounds. Look at her long."

I don't know how long I kept looking at the moon as it ascended, but I remember hearing Sinffi saying as if from a far distance: "She is going to draw you out of me tonight, brother, so that I will not have to carry you with me forever. I will be free once again. But you remember the two stars."

I'm sure that Sinffi Cooper stopped the clock in Spetchley Wood that night, because when I took my eyes off the moon, she had gone. The dawn chorus was starting and the sky was lighting over Bredon. I walked in a deze towards the place where the gypsy camp was, but there was no one there. The *vardos* had gone; there was only the black fire circle left. There was no sign of the *patrin* either — the short grass and sticks that Sinffi left sometimes on the ground to point her path.

I let myself down against the tree stump where she had so often sat to shell peas. If the moonlight had brought any relief to her feelings, it had done precious little for mine.

I rose and walked without purpose across country from field to wood — I don't know exactly where — and the hedges and the water, the sun and the wind were full of Sinffi Cooper, and in these things she dwelt for a long time after.